What Makes a Good School Now?

Also available from Network Continuum

Inspirations – Tim Brighouse and David Woods

Distributing Leadership for Personalizing Learning – Ron Ritchie and
  Ruth Deakin Crick

Learn to Transform – David Crossley and Graham Corbyn

Tweak to Transform – Mike Hughes

Available from Continuum

How to Run Your School Successfully – Adrian Percival and Susan Tranter

How to Improve Your School – Jean Rudduck and Julia Flutter

What Makes a Good School Now?

Tim Brighouse and David Woods

network
continuum

Network Continuum.
An imprint of Continuum.

Continuum International Publishing Group

The Tower Building   80 Maiden Lane, Suite 704
11 York Road   New York, NY 10038
London
SE1 7NX

www.continuumbooks.com
www.networkpress.co.uk

British Library Cataloguing-in-Publication Data
A catalogue record for this book is available from the British Library.

ISBN: 9781855390843 (paperback)

Library of Congress Cataloging-in-Publication Data
Brighouse, Tim.
  What makes a good school now? / Tim Brighouse and David Woods.
     p. cm.
  Includes bibliographical references and index.
  ISBN 978-1-85539-084-3
  1. School improvement programs—Great Britain. 2. Educational leadership—Great Britain. I. Woods, David, 1942- II. Title.
  LB2822.84.G7B758 2008
  371.200973—dc22
                         2007044342
Typeset by Ben Cracknell Studios | www.benstudios.co.uk
Printed and bound in Great Britain by Cromwell Press, Wiltshire.

179105788

Contents

List of Abbreviations and Glossary

BTEC	Business and Technicians' Education Council
BSF	Building Schools for the Future
CLT	chartered London teacher
CPD	continuous professional development
DCSF	Department for Children, Schools and Families
DfES	Department for Education and Skills
EAL	English as an additional language
GNVQ	General National Vocational Qualification
GTC	General Teaching Council
HE	Higher Education
INSET days	Non-teaching days, formerly known as Baker days (after their instigator) and sometimes referred to as occasional or professional development days
LA	local authority
LEA	local education authority
LMS	local management of schools
PGCE	Postgraduate Certificate of Education
QCA	Qualification and Curriculum Authority
RSA	Royal Society of Arts
SAT	standard assessment task
SCITT	School Consortium for Initial Training
SEF	school evaluation form
SIPs	school improvement partners
TDA	Training and Development Agency
TES	*Times Educational Supplement*
TLA	teaching and learning allowance
TLR	teaching and learning responsibility
VAK	visual, auditory and kinaesthetic

Preface

When I wrote the first version of this book 15 years ago I was at Keele University, after ten years running Oxfordshire's education service and more than half a lifetime in and around schools. A formative experience in my childhood left me fascinated as to why some schools are much more successful than others. At Keele I had the opportunity to read extensively about this subject, and I set up one or two small research projects into what caused school success or failure to happen. I was helped in writing *What Makes a Good School?* by numerous colleagues at Keele, but especially by Mike Johnson. He pioneered 'student and staff surveys', which even then we could see as a powerful means of promoting school improvement, and which today are still not used as often as they should be, or to their full potential. Indeed, they could provide a very timely balance to the attainment-driven means of holding schools accountable that we now deploy in league tables and Ofsted.

Since the book's original publication, however, I have learned much more. I've spent a decade as Birmingham's chief education officer where I met David Woods, who as chief adviser was instrumental in the early successes of an education service that had been unfairly dubbed by the Secretary of State as 'the worst in the country'. Now it is generally recognized – for the comparative data allows no other conclusion – that the transformation in the overall standards of educational attainment outcomes is remarkable. People beat a path to the city to see how it happened. Much of the improvement continued after we had left, and in any case the answer is simple: that there are more outstanding school staff and schools than there were. More youngsters have more moments when they are accessing something of significance.

The remaining five years since the first edition have been spent as chief adviser to London's schools as part of a government-funded London Challenge intended to act as a catalyst in transforming first London's secondary schools and, more recently, the primary schools. I was joined in that endeavour by David, who had been leading the DfES school-effectiveness team.

Whenever I met the publisher of *What Makes a Good School?* he would badger me about an updated version. This is what David and I have attempted. Much of the original is still relevant but, of course, there has been so much change in context. We've learned much more about school improvement and about teaching, learning and assessment. So, this version is very different. After all, I wrote in 1991 that 'The 1980s were unsettled times: union power was exercised in a period of great disturbance and one bewildering set of legislation was quickly followed by another affecting variously governance, pay, funding, curriculum and exams.'

How modest that change looks now. In 1991 the National Curriculum had barely reached the end of Key Stage 1 and local management of schools was not fully implemented. There were no Ofsted regular inspections and they didn't involve reporting to parents, still less writing to children. It was an age before league tables – whether of the raw score variety or the added value and contextual added value embellishments. It was before the substantial and continuing changes to the ill-thought-through National Curriculum, the discussions and proposals for 14–19 education, the *Every Child Matters* agenda, let alone 'personalization', 'teaching and learning responsibilities' and workforce reform. Local education authorities have been discontinued and children's departments have been created in local authorities. National Strategies bestride the scene and schools are learning to work with their 'school-improvement partners' and exploring whether they can prove effective as 'extended schools'. Meanwhile a new National College of School Leadership wrestles with the problems of supplying a sufficient flow of well-trained, next-generation school leaders.

We can be sure that in 15 years time this roll-call of change will itself look careworn. What David and I have done is to select concepts from the first edition and add other ideas from our work together. We shall introduce to you the idea of 'butterflies' and material from *Essential Pieces: The jigsaw of a successful school* (2006) and *How to Improve Your School* (1999), as well as other pieces we have written either together or separately. We have tried to avoid it being a 'cut, paste and copy' exercise by drawing in new material and discussing at length whether we really think material is relevant to practitioners or merely interesting.

Our intended audience is not academics but busy school leaders and staff, and perhaps interested governors as well as, of course, SIPs – that lovely acronym for 'school-improvement partners'.

Finally, we would like to thank all the headteachers, teachers and school staff with whom we have worked over the years, especially in Birmingham, London, Solihull and Oxfordshire, but also others we have met all over the country. We also owe a debt of gratitude to Max Tavinor for technical assistance and particularly to Gina Henderson, who has been so patient and cheerfully efficient in helping us to put the manuscript together. Thanks are also due to Tracey O'Brien of Southfields Community College, London, and Sue Barrett of Bournville Junior School in Birmingham for their help.

Tim Brighouse
January 2008

Introduction

A definition and consideration of 'success'

As we said in the Preface, this book is intended to help all those who, in their everyday work, are trying to make schools ever more successful.

So what is a successful school? How would you recognize one? Does it necessarily have school uniform or dress and is there an honours board? Do you need to see the exam results? Is it defined by sporting success? Where do those excellent musical productions fit in? If you think it is all those things, how do you recognize success in primary schools or a special school?

Is it also to be affirmed or denied by the views of the people in the school's locality, the shopkeepers in the town centre or the local employers? Is it to be won or lost by the messages and views of the staff who happen not to be teachers at the school – the caretaker, the secretary, the technician, the learning mentor, the teaching assistant, the school meals staff, or the parents or governors? Is it to be seen in the behaviour of the children?

Is there a way of comparing the success of the school in a prosperous, leafy middle-class area with another school in a deprived inner city, or a school in the south with one in the north? The questions crowd in.

Unlike a company with a profit-and-loss account, a school's balance-sheet is more difficult to read and it may not show up in any case until years later. How do you take into account events such as that raised in a letter from a London teacher: 'One of my Year 9 girls has just started to read after six months of our mutual struggle. The moment was indescribable: she is walking on air and we have shouted our joy from the rooftops.'

Some things are clear. If 30 per cent of the pupils at the age of 11 cannot read their own language, if there are pupil exclusions every week, if the staff turnover is very high, if there are fights everyday in the playground, if there is no pupils' work displayed in the classroom or if it has been there all year, if the teacher cannot tell you about promising signs in the development of each and every pupil in their classroom, you have got problems.

If 80 per cent of students leave school with E, F or G grades, or none at all, if there are very few extracurricular activities, if the library is empty of students and the computer suites are not in use before school, in the lunch hours and after school, if the musical instruments are lost or broken, if the absentee rate in the fifth year (Year 11) is 30 per cent, if there is a high incidence of staff sickness, you have found a disaster. It is very short odds that the staff in such schools are miserable. Ask yourself the question whether you would send your child to either of those schools and then whether you believe that group of researchers who claim that schools don't make a difference?

This book starts from an entirely different set of assumptions. First, and unequivocally, we believe from close observation over 40 years that schools *do* make a difference, that they have a massive effect on children's life chances, whatever their background, for good or ill. We pity the thousands of children who go through school without experiencing a worthwhile relationship with at least one teacher: they have not really been at school.

Second, the book makes the assumption that those involved in every school will want to make it a successful place; that if you scratch hard enough, all staff, when they are appointed to their post in the school, will reveal a dream or a vision of how things could be in their classroom and in their school.

This book has the word 'good' in its title to quantify the school we seek to describe – yet we prefer 'successful'. In any case the word 'good' has been called into question by Ofsted's four-point rating that attributes to 'good' the qualitative of 'second-class'. In their parlance we are seeking 'outstanding'. Schools should be places where everyone of its community tastes the confidence that comes with success in some form or other. Every youngster ought to be entitled to attend a successful school. In any case, it is very much more rewarding for adults to work in a successful school.

Indeed, for teachers the quest to improve becomes more urgent. That fickle weather-vane 'parental choice' is championed by all politicians, and the position of schools in the local league table becomes more important. Ofsted too may come visiting, along with their redefinitions of the word 'satisfactory', which in reality means 'unsatisfactory'.

A framework: a process

We spent many years championing a framework of school processes which, if we learn ever more about each of them, is likely to help any school get better.

- *Leading at every level* – while recognizing the need for different styles in different circumstances and at different times.
- *Managing* – again at different levels, ensuring that everyone plays their part in getting the detail right.
- *Creating a fit environment* – visually, aurally, behaviourally and in a way that encourages learning.
- *Learning, teaching and assessing* – the bread, butter and jam of schooling. It occupies everyone's time.
- *Developing staff* – not just teachers but all staff, by making sound appointments, providing thorough inductions and extensive further professional development, which combines individual and collective need.
- *Self-evaluating and critically reviewing* – an activity that prompts gradual or great change and which is now back centre-stage after some years in the shadows.

- *Involving and connecting with parents and the community* – often overlooked, but key if the public place that is the school is to be accessible to all who might benefit and contribute.

We would advocate a focus on learning even more about these processes. As a guiding compass and map as we pioneered new territory in school improvement, it has proved invaluable. Through developing and researching case-studies, writers – above all, practitioners doing the job – have widened our understanding of each of these processes or some close variation of the process map.

In considering these processes we want school to be a place where:

- All talk of 'our' achievement and everyone is anxious to improve on their own and shared achievement.
- All pupils are increasingly aware of their potential and that it is without limit if they make the effort.
- Everyone feels fulfilled in what they do and contributes to the fulfilment of others.
- The full range of success – sporting, academic, artistic, practical support for others, triumph over adversity – is celebrated.
- All members of the school community are committed to their own continuous learning and support that of others.
- Everyone is aware of the school's collective past and present success and is ambitious to contribute to that collective legacy for future generations.
- Nobody is in fear of physical or emotional abuse.
- The school is there to facilitate these aims and to promote the fun of learning and the pleasure of achievement.

Context is everything

We believe that the context – of people, organizational size, time and place – is everything.

People

The headteacher, as the chapter on leadership will demonstrate, is a key influence. Consider the following case-study:

Case-study

'Absolutely useless' was the education officer's verdict. Yet at the time and ever since this comment puzzled me.

The judgement was passed in the early 1990s on a headteacher of a school in sharp decline in reputation, in numbers – indeed in any indicator of measurable achievement. Everything told the same depressing story: the staff turnover rates had suddenly escalated so that there were either the very young who were escaping at the first opportunity or the very old waiting for early retirement. The strong mid-career head of department in the mid-30s to early 40s, who had been a feature of the school's heyday, had moved on soon after the new head had arrived. They were not replaced by the same calibre of able and heavily committed teachers who had been excellent role models not merely for the students but also for the younger staff. On the contrary, the jobs had gone to poor appointees either from within or outside.

There was other corroborating evidence. The exclusion rate was going up; the education welfare service was reporting an increased workload from truancy; the peripatetic musicians had few clients. The head's analysis of the exam results to the governors was beginning to vary from year to year in order to emphasize the features of success and conceal the acknowledged widening areas of failure. Staying on post-16 was steady, but dropout rates after the first year of sixth form told a sorry story.

The governors were collectively loyal and unquestioning, but privately and individually alarmed and looking, as they always do in such circumstances, to the authority to do something. There was no question about it – one of the authority's more successful schools was in decline. Only the design and technology department continued to shine under the leadership of a robust head of department, an engagingly self-motivated renaissance woman, with interests far beyond the school and a productivity and work-rate which made mere mortals breathless.

Success in one headship is no guarantee of success in different circumstances.

The headteacher had been a head before, apparently with a proven successful record, confirmed not just by the conventional referencing system but by double-checks through the network of previous working connections that the authority regularly used to vet key appointments.

It was a case-study that confirmed two truths: the first, that it is impossible to have a good and successful school without a successful leader, is well known; the second less so, namely that having been a successful leader once is no guarantee that you will be so again, either in the same place or elsewhere.

Since that time of course, Ofsted reports, the impact of league tables and parental choice and the attention to annual data of one sort or another means that 'plateauing' or 'decline' in a school can be spotted and occur more quickly than before. It does not invalidate the proposition that success in one place is no guarantee of success in another. The 'second-time-around' head can take fatal short cuts in his early days, taking for granted that his previous reputation – which of course is totally unknown to the new school community – will mean he'll get the benefit of the doubt in a crisis that he would have received in his first school. Too many incidents of this sort can quickly undermine collective confidence.

We shall turn to the key process that this issue implies – namely the appointment of staff and heads – later. First let's turn to the three other important contextual variables.

Size of organization

> Running a small school or department may not help in running a large one.

It used to be thought in Oxfordshire, as in other shire counties, that a promising young primary teacher should first serve his/her probation successfully as a headteacher of a two-, three- or four-teacher village school, before aspiring to one of the few larger primary schools. The policy originated in the need to revitalize the many small rural primary schools after the Second World War when, previously, they had often been staffed by unqualified teachers.

It was part of the pioneering policy and practice of a down-to-earth but charismatic northerner called Edith Moorhouse, who made Oxfordshire and successful primary practice synonymous. A quarter of a century on, in a less deferential and more changeable age, the policy was careworn. She, but not her successors, would have recognized the changed circumstances.

It was not merely a logistical issue, although this needed to be considered, since clearly if there were many more small primary schools than larger ones (which there tend to be in rural areas) it seemed inevitable that some appointed young would grow old in their proving ground! In fact the logistical issue was not really a problem because Oxfordshire's primary teachers benefited from Edith Moorhouse's success in the sense that to have served in Oxfordshire gave applicants for headship elsewhere in the country an edge, so that those who really wanted to move on to jobs with wider responsibilities could always do so if they were ambitious. It was more to do with the obvious point – that to run a small school was not necessarily a good or sufficient training for running a larger school.

The size and range of the relationships that have to be sustained in primary schools with 10–15 teachers and half as many again other staff, not to mention 300–400 pupils and their parents, is many, many times greater than in a three- or four-teacher primary school with 70 pupils and parents in a settled community where the seasons impose a rhythm of their own.

Therefore, the experience gained as deputy or in a post of responsibility in a school environment comparable to that for which a candidate is an applicant may be important. It is not that people cannot make the transition: simply that it is important that they show at interview, and in practice, their realization that leadership in a small-school environment is quite different from a larger one. Clearly if there is a finite number of interest groups who have a legitimate call on the leader's time, the larger the number in any group, the more the leader needs to reflect on the best way of organizing her time in order that each individual receives the attention he or she deserves.

The example is not confined to primary schools. To run a secondary school of 500 students is a different proposition from running a school of 800, and that is different again from running one with over 1,200 students. Indeed, at that point the complexity is of an order that begins to demand a subtlety of leadership skills and a deep sensitive understanding of those issues. Such qualities are rare. The jobs are simply quite different.

A headteacher I know and admire in a three-form entry school decided to transform expectations of students and staff. This was a priority that admitted for him only one answer. He would take over the teaching of history himself. He burned the midnight oil, rewrote the schemes of work and allowed nothing to come between him and his teaching of the fourth and fifth year. It paid off and was preceded by, and coupled with, a sharp and shared analysis of GCSE performances of the same students in different subjects across the whole age range. Results are improving in the wake of consistently higher expectations, and to the head's relief – he harbours a refreshing sense of self-doubt – the history results have helped prove the point. The outcome has been successful.

In discussing the tactic the head acknowledged that to effect the same outcome by the same tactics in a school twice the size would not have been possible. Given the intensity of obligations in a large establishment, he would have tackled the issue differently. Interestingly – and it would be convincing to me if I were interviewing him for a post in a larger school – he showed an ability to identify a key issue and appreciate the imperative of size. As it happens, this particular individual has worked in a variety of different sized schools. The same considerations apply, though with less urgency, to heads of departments or to those leading pastoral teams or infant or junior departments, or upper or lower schools with different sized groups.

Time and place

Success in one part of the country is no guarantee of success elsewhere.

Leadership of schools today calls for similar qualities and skills as those required a generation ago: it is just that the circumstances in which they are exercised make higher demands. Society is more loosely coupled and assumptions about parents, staff and governors evidently have changed.

Some of the general factors have a sharply focused local emphasis; for example a multi-faith and faithless society, greater divisions between rich and poor, increased homelessness and a sharp increase in one-parent families. Other factors apply everywhere; the increased emphasis on rights and less on responsibility, the emphasis on parental choice and an increased application of market forces within education, together with the need to handle the huge externally imposed agenda of change.

Finally by way of introductory explanation we know that good and purposeful story telling, as well as questioning and explanation – all coupled with imagery, metaphor and simile – are part of the stock-in-trade both of school leaders and their teaching staff.

The culture associated with particular regions of the country, however, is another contextual factor. A person who understands the nuances of the north-east may not have recognized a dependence on a natural affinity for the folklore of the people and their schools' traditions. Success in one part of the country is no guarantee of success elsewhere. Similarly, a leader who fails in an urban setting may not be unsuccessful in a rural one, although interestingly the reverse is less likely to be true. Some headteachers, who are naturally expert and proficient in taking by the scruff of the neck the school in decline and shaking it into a new sense of purpose and direction, are absolutely useless in sustaining a school already enjoying the fruits of success. Here the call is for the more subtle skill of sustaining the highest possible rate of change and improvement without allowing it to accelerate unsustainably or drift towards complacency.

Schools are places where remembered successes and a sense of history can so easily become ancient rather than modern. Some leaders are successful in expansion but useless in contraction: others the reverse. There are separate and identifiable skills associated with the leadership and management of all these different situations.

To say, therefore, that all schools are unique is a truism: each is serving a subtly or widely different community. The variables, as we have seen, include the background of the pupils (race, socioeconomic status, faith) and the community it serves (in an affluent area, in an area of social challenge or on a good communication route so that it may draw its pupils from far and wide). The school may be at the top or the bottom of the pecking-order of schools, or be somewhere in the middle; in consequence it will have more, or fewer, pupils who have done well at their Key Stage SATs. It may, or may not, suffer from excessive mobility of pupils and staff. It may have a financial deficit or falling numbers. It may, or may not, be able to draw on external sources of money or expertise. And of course, every school is at a different point in the trajectory of its journey; it may be on the way up or declining. Or, to confuse matters further, it may be a mixture of both according to the staffing in different departments.

Our book contains butterflies

There is, however, one idiosyncratic addition that requires explanation: the 'butterfly'. We first came across them in Birmingham where we were impressed by the little school practices, sometimes context-dependent, which seemed to have a disproportionate impact on school success. Let us begin to explain. David Hargreaves distinguishes two kinds of practice or intervention. 'Low leverage' interventions are familiar – a lot of effort goes into the new practice and pay-off is paltry. The contrast is with 'high leverage' interventions: relatively low effort to formulate or implement, but yielding extremely beneficial outcomes in terms of learning and ethos. All school leaders aim to avoid low leverage practices, and find high leverage alternatives. We believe all schools are capable, whether through helpful external consultancy and advice or critical self-evaluation, of turning from low to high leverage practices. Those that are successful in doing so are those that will improve.

That's where the 'butterfly effect' comes in. In the spirit of seeking high leverage, both in the important things in school life and in reinforcing how the important things are done, we believe that small interventions can have a disproportionate effect. We call them 'butterflies' after the chaos or complexity theorist's story that if sufficient butterflies were to beat their wings in the Amazonian forest they could trigger a hurricane thousands of miles away. High leverage indeed – but sometimes, if you were to put yourself in the position of the butterfly, quite a lot of effort.

In Chapter 2 we explain how schools themselves can create energy and improvement by collecting their own butterflies from their own practice.

1 Leading towards success

Leadership is to the current decade what standards were to the 1990s for those interested in large-scale reform. Standards, even when well implemented, can take us only part way to large-scale reform. It is only leadership that can take us all the way.

Michael Fullan (2003)

Leadership and learnership are indispensable to one another.

Attributed to John F. Kennedy

There is a difference between leadership and management. Leadership is of the spirit, compounded of personality and vision; its practice is an art. Management is of the mind, a matter of accurate calculation . . . its practice is a science. Managers are necessary; leaders are essential.

Field Marshal Lord Slim, quoted in Van Maurik (2001)

Leadership is ambiguous

The qualities of school leaders, particularly headteachers, and how they deploy their competencies are widely acknowledged to be the key ingredients to school success. Without the right combination of them, researchers agree that they've never come across a truly successful school.

Xenophon described the required qualities of the elected general as: 'Ingenious, energetic, careful, full of stamina and presence of mind . . . loving and tough, straightforward and craft, ready to gamble everything and wishing to have everything, generous and greedy, trusting and suspicious.'

The military is perhaps an inappropriate analogy for headship. Would Napoleon, both decisive and prepared to add to and modify plans if somebody came along with a better idea, have made a good head? We suspect not. The point is that heads have to handle 'ambiguity': once they are comfortable with that, they will relax into the job. Not, as some people say a lonely one, but full of relationship-building and maintenance . . . and so busy, that there's no time to feel alone.

Leadership, management and administration

There is a world of difference between 'leadership' and 'management': the first is primarily to do with planning and vision and the second with organization and provision. They are not, of course, neatly discrete and they impinge one on the other. There is probably a cycle in the running of any organization of planning, organizing, providing, maintaining, monitoring, evaluating and further planning (see Figure 1).

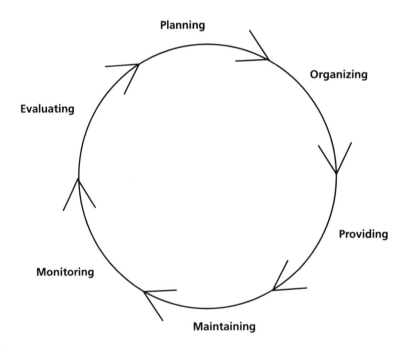

Figure 1 Cycle of running an organization

It is very important, and a feature of long-term success, that the leadership of an organization secures the effective discharge of all parts of this cycle. The smaller the institution, the more it is necessary for one person to incorporate within his/her own personal functioning an ability to lead, manage and administer. In a large and complex school, it is on the other hand crucial to know *who* is doing *what* tasks *when*, and who has *responsibility* for the tasks.

Some heads are instinctively strong on planning, monitoring and evaluating. For example, they produce or enable others to produce most impressive long-term development plans: in doing so they go for highly participative, collective review in order to ensure a high degree of ownership for the direction in which the school is then determined to proceed. They plan the collection of evidence and promise the review of the various new directions to which they are committed. Unfortunately they may not be so good at organizing and making provision for those variables such as time, books and equipment, which allow the new changes to be introduced effectively.

Others may do all of that but overlook the small detailed administrative support essential to the smooth running of any activity. The everyday back-up in the school office and technicians' workshops is crucial to curriculum and organizational change, both in the school as a whole and in faculties and departments.

For other leaders, the attraction and emphases may lie differently. In a one-, two- or three-teacher primary school, it is probably inevitable that one has to live with the combination of strengths and weaknesses that is the profile of the one individual. People outside can do their best by coaching to help their head or head of department compensate for their weaker suit, but they are unlikely to do more than that.

In the medium-sized school – and by that we mean anything up to 1,000 students – it should be possible for any senior management team of heads, deputies and senior colleagues to analyse honestly their complementary strengths and weaknesses and ensure that leadership, management and administration are exercised both overall and in the separate areas (for example in staff development, external relations, curriculum development, assessment systems and so on). Detailed leadership, therefore, is exercised by different people in these different facets of school life.

When people talk about *responsibility* in the context of school life, they are usually talking about the chance to exercise leadership. For example, a new member of staff may be 'taking the lead' in a curriculum development: the phrase must imply initiative and taking responsibility when things need to be done in order to see that aims are accomplished. If, however, the work they do is ignored and no one shows interest in its development, if it is taken for granted, the school is always in danger of slipping from a position of 'positive development' to that of 'systems maintenance' and to eventual decline.

The example below illustrates this:

A main-scale teacher in a small secondary school is charged with taking the lead on parents'/school policy issues. She produces a report that analyses the various interactions between school and parents: social (PTA), educational (homework/reporting on students' progress), governmental (governing bodies/parents' educational evenings) and makes proposals for change and new developments.

If the leadership of the school has not thought through the organizational ways of providing for the changes and subsequently maintaining them, or ignores the recommendations in this respect from the staff member, an enormous drain of energy and enthusiasm will occur in the interest and commitment of the staff member whose initiative is so ignored. Worse still, of course, will be the irritation to other members of staff if the initiative is improperly planned or in competition with another priority.

Typically, however, the greater danger lies in the scheme getting off the ground and then no one from the school leadership showing sufficient or sustained interest in the tender new plant or its need both for continued but carefully measured support and appreciation, and for well-timed, critical review.

What this example shows is the failure of the leaders of the school to manage the opportunity they have given another to lead properly. They have stopped short with the chance they originally gave to teachers to take a lead by not translating it from the planning phase to actual experience of leadership in action. *Good management is the essential handmaiden of leadership.*

Some people believe there is a tension between leadership and management – that somehow one is better than the other. They are, however, complementary: you need both. We were impressed by the comment from a management consultant (whose comments we hasten to add don't invariably impress) that 'most UK organizations are underled and overmanaged. There is only one thing worse, namely organizations that are overled and undermanaged.'

Transformation or transaction? Or both?

We came across a collection of points and counterpoints describing transformational and transactional leaders that, in its value-laden way, is set out in Table 1. There are many points in the right-hand, 'transactional', column that are desirable within any organization. However, there are some that are not. It is not simply doing the right thing; it's often necessary for the smooth running of an organization like a school to do things right. Despite the validity of some of the statements in the right-hand column of the table, we suspect that they were put together by someone keener on leadership than management of the necessarily transactional type.

LEADERSHIP	
TRANSFORMATIONAL	**TRANSACTIONAL**
Builds on the need for meaning.	Builds on need to get the job done and make a living.
Preoccupied with purposes, values, morals and ethics.	Preoccupied with power and position, politics and perks.
Transcends daily affairs.	Swamped in daily affairs.
Oriented towards long-term goals without compromising human values and principles.	Oriented to short-term goals and hard data.
Separates causes and symptoms and works at prevention.	Confuses causes and symptoms and is concerned with treatment.
Aligns internal structures and systems to reinforce overarching values and goals.	Supports structures and systems that reinforce the bottom line.
Focuses more on missions and strategies for achieving them.	Focuses on tactical issues.
Makes full use of available resources (human).	Relies on human relationship to oil human interactions.
Designs and redesigns jobs to make them meaningful and challenging; realizes human potential.	Follows and fulfils role expectations by striving to work effectively within current systems.

Table 1 The differences between transformational and transactional leadership

Management systems support leadership. For example, both the staff handbook and job-descriptions can be couched in language that straddles both management and leadership. We cover the detail of that in Chapter 2.

Qualities and characteristics of leadership

We started this chapter with a reference to the need of the leader to live with ambiguity and, half seriously, included a quotation from Xenophon. Successful school leaders, however, will model in their behaviour a set of values that commands the respect of staff who, like them, believe in the unlimited potential and future capabilities of all their pupils. Unlike generals, they create and construct rather than fight and destroy.

There is no single successful style of leader of course. Some are naturally extrovert, others introvert: both styles of leadership are successful. The key common ingredient is integrity: how you speak, who you are and how you are perceived to act need to match. You know exactly where the successful leader stands.

As PricewaterhouseCoopers (2007) showed in their recent study of school leadership, teachers and support staff value those factors set out below.

> Effective leaders:
> - adopt an open, consultative and non-hierarchical approach – distribute leadership responsibilities effectively
> - are approachable and visible throughout the school
> - communicate effectively with all staff
> - take performance management of staff seriously, and provide clear development pathways for staff
> - understand classroom practice as well as the role of the school in the wider community.

Whether one is leading in a classroom, in a faculty or the whole school, it's essential to have energy, enthusiasm and hope. We use 'hope', not 'optimism', because there is the promise of delivery: it's a matter of determination, not opinion. When someone said that teachers and headteachers needed 'unwarranted optimism', that's what they are getting at. Leaders will regard crisis as the norm and complexity as fun. They will experience a lot of both. They need an endless well of intellectual curiosity to feed speculation about what's possible, to keep asking questions rather than continually provide the answers. Finally, they need a complete absence of paranoia and self-pity. As a leader, whether of maths or the whole school, you are credited with seeing further and wider on that topic than others. You make coherence. To make coherence of the leaders of maths or English and so on, the head needs to listen and put her expert knowledge about maths or English together in a wider context – the local community, the national changes, the turnover of staff and students, the availability of resources. Vitally, she fits this into a view of the future that translates into a collective vision for the school community.

As we have already said, people need to know where their leaders are coming from so far as values are concerned. So many teachers say they admire the effort, commitment and energy, the sheer hard work, openness and good intentions of leaders, where a school or department is thought successful and is brought face to face with the real importance of excellence. Hard work, however, is only forgiven if people know where their leaders are coming from so far as values are concerned. That is probably why the researchers say that leadership is most successful after three years because until then, especially in the large institutions, it is difficult to know what makes the leader tick and therefore inevitably different decisions about personal cases will make giving the benefit of the doubt more difficult.

Like the outstanding teacher, the headteacher also demonstrates and communicates a belief that all youngsters can be successful. Consequently their view of intelligence is not mean-spirited or narrow. Like the American Howard Gardner, they believe that there are many forms of intelligence and that each can be increased in every individual. They want all their pupils to acquire a love of learning that will last a lifetime – and demonstrate their own lifetime learning habits as a model.

There is one last point about leadership that demands notice: perhaps it is the most important of all. It has been said that one of the key features of a successful school is the number of rewarding relationships a pupil has with teachers. There is much in that proposition. Certainly if a pupil has no meaningful relationship with any teacher, one does feel sorry for them . . . it will be unlikely that school will have been much use to them.

So also it is with leadership. Within the department and the school, pity the teacher who finds no one to whom they can relate with relaxation and confidence in a personal and professional way. If there were a litmus test of leadership, it would probably incorporate a way of assessing how the staff saw the trust, confidence and humour factors among the senior members of the leadership team of the school.

Inevitably, however much the process is shared (as it should be) the leader in a large organization cannot be in continuous touch with the various stakeholders. They will make regular systematic contact, replete with acts of unexpected kindness and thoughtfulness, but the contact cannot be constant. It is essential that at times of crisis the leader digs deep into determination and doesn't fall prey to self-pity.

Although we know that the qualities of integrity and commitment will get a headteacher a long way, they do need some everyday skills and some overarching ones too.

Everyday skills

In the medium-to-large school or department, headteachers would argue that teamwork can secure the complementary development of people's particular strengths. So, for example, my optimism can be enhanced by your better sense of the use of time. Leaders get subtly steered or steer themselves into the activities they are good at, but they should never forget that they will need to deploy their own personal, weaker areas from time to time in a crisis, so they need to work very hard to improve their less successful characteristics or skills. Skills of taking a meeting, of writing a paper or presenting an argument are all activities that can be improved over time.

The successful leader realizes this. Some heads and head of departments do not chair important meetings or working groups but merely attend as one member, albeit acknowledged tacitly as a very important member. Others chair all the meetings. Some write many influential papers for those meetings; others rarely do so and when they do, only on the basis of efforts drafted by others and only marginally amended.

Still on the question of context: meetings must take place somewhere. But the *time* and the *place* are important, A cramped, badly ventilated classroom at the end of a busy week, with no refreshments, where people cannot see each other, is clearly not as propitious as comfortable surroundings with a known closing time, perhaps for a prearranged purpose involving the celebration of some staff efforts and accompanied by food and drink.

Staff meetings remain a trap for the best leaders and managers, whether departmentally or at school level. Once again, the larger the meeting the more hazardous the situation. Meetings too must have a purpose and their regularity should not be dictated by a calendar that is the theft of time, but by necessity.

So 'every half-term', 'every month', 'every fortnight', 'every week', 'every day' are phrases that betray, with an escalating sense of desperation, an unconsidered use of valuable time and probably sow the seeds of irritation and exhaustion for leader and led alike. The more successful leaders have considered the following questions for meetings:

- How often are the meetings really necessary?
- Am I consulting or informing and do we all know which it is?
- Is there an agenda?
- Are participants consulted on prospective items?
- Are there sufficient items for the meeting to go ahead?
- Is the agenda circulated?
- Are items timed?
- Who is to write a brief action sheet as a follow-up?
- Are these action sheets to be made widely available?
- Who are the potential allies at the meeting and who needs to be brought into the debate?
- Who needs to be present and who can be present?

The 'manager', which must lurk under every teacher's skin, gives the most careful attention to all forms of communication and is keenly aware that these need analysis and evaluation from time to time. The most successful leaders change their style in the matter of communication and meetings, in order that familiarity does not dull the perceptions that they have of the school and its activities. Of course, they remain constant in their values although they vary their habits.

If, however, there are skills that are deployed in the processes of leadership and management, they are not exercised in a mechanical or depersonalized way: to each task and activity leaders bring their own qualities, talents or intelligences. Probably of all the attributes leaders need, the ability to understand themselves, and themselves in relation to others, has never been more important.

Apart from these everyday skills we have already identified, there are probably three overarching ones in which leaders should be proficient:

- delegation
- managing change
- using time to optimum effect.

The nine levels of delegation

1 Look into this problem. Give me all the facts. I will decide what to do.
2 Let me know the options available, with the pros and cons of each. I will decide what to select.
3 Let me know the criteria for your recommendation, which alternatives you have identified and which one appears best to you, with any risk identified. I will make the decision.
4 Recommend a course of action for my approval.
5 Let me know what you intend to do. Delay action until I approve.
6 Let me know what you intend to do. Do it unless I say not to.
7 Take action. Let me know what you did. Let me know how it turns out.
8 Take action. Communicate with me only if action is unsuccessful.
9 Take action. No further communication with me is necessary.

The list above sets out the possible positions when determining how and when to delegate. Clearly, as we relax or revert to type, we will all have our preferred position, but we will have learned the skill of deliberately deciding where to be on the spectrum of possible positions with different people for different tasks. You may feel that someone new in a job will require some support as they adjust to new surroundings but decide later that they are at, for example, 7, 8 or 9 for most things. Indeed you'd be bothered if you needed to be at 2, 3 or 4 – desperate if you needed to be at 1!

Being aware of this spectrum is therefore a helpful guide to the need for extended professional development for others – or oneself.

One final word of caution about delegation. The surest way of consuming energy and demotivating or disempowering staff is to tell them they are at 7 but at the height of a crisis or in external matters regret it too late and tell them subsequently they are at 5!

Managing change

Hoffer (1998) once said, 'In times of change the learners inherit the earth whilst the learned find themselves beautifully equipped to deal with a world that no longer exists.'

Teachers of today understand that. Increasing numbers of young and old alike can use the internet to become well informed about any particular topic; 20 years ago visits to libraries were restricted. What is more, the 'deferential' age has given way to the more 'disputatious' and 'participative' present day.

The teacher is no longer, if she ever was, the sole supplier of information. Rather the teacher is the coach, the developer of pupils' skills and competence, as well as the wise and trusted guide on values and where to go for further information. She knows that to learn is to change.

However, the present day has brought incessant externally imposed change from successive central governments. The successful school sees to it that every member of staff understands some of the essentials of change, so they can welcome it, divert it or resist it as the school community decides. The successful school will have inwardly registered some of the rules of change.

The first lesson concerns complex change. Table 2 shows what happens when any one of five essential ingredients is absent. Of course, it doesn't explain the dysfunctionality that is created when two or three are absent or when all you've got is a succession of 'action plans' with no vision, skills, resources or incentives! However, it's a helpful guide to implementing change.

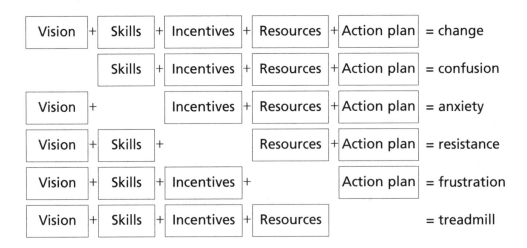

Figure 2 Managing complex change
Source: Adapted from Knoster (1991) Presentation at TASH Conference, Washington DC (Adapted in turn by Knoster from Enterprise Group Ltd)

'Internally generated change' is always welcome. It arises from members of the school community, perhaps in a school improvement group, suggesting change and having it adopted. 'Externally available change' is the sort of change that you can embrace and tailor to your needs. It might be a behaviour system or in curricular terms, the *Opening Minds* project of the RSA. This, too, is welcome. 'Externally mandated change' is much more difficult. All these sorts demand attention to the subtle management of complex change.

Most importantly, welcoming change involves knowing that 'if a thing's worth doing it's worth doing badly', the first time round during the adoption phrase. Of course, second time round, after review, 'it's worth doing better'. Finally, in the consolidation phrase, anything 'is worth doing well'. There are 'change rules' concerned with who is put in charge, support groups and review.

Anyone serious about this piece of the jigsaw will want to read Michael Fullan's books, either the popular easy read *Leading in a Culture of Change* (2001) or the more theoretical *The New Meaning of Educational Change* (1991).

Using time to optimum effect

Leaders remind themselves that when anyone is with them it is important that the person believes themselves to be the most important in the world at that time. Some colleagues we have known well have displayed an enviable strength in this respect.

Listening skills can be improved or inhibited. For instance, the clock on the wall behind the guest's chair is often too much of a temptation for many of us to resist. So too is the wristwatch. One of the arts of leaders is to give the impression of leisureliness, even amid their frantic programme. They should be able to control the length of a conversation without the sense of urgency that distracted glances inevitably convey. 'I can give you five minutes' is a comment that has its place, but only rarely.

Headteachers too can ensure that there are opportunities for casual conversation: they will occur in regular, unobtrusive but natural visits to the staffroom or dining area. Leaders will consider the natural habitats of their various constituents in order to supplement whatever may be the formal communication meetings in the patterns of school life. Inevitably, the teaching and support staff of the school are a very high priority so far as listening is concerned. There are many other legitimate constituents of a headteacher: the parents, the pupils themselves, the governors, the local community, the local authority's officers and advisers, not to mention the very important forum of fellow headteachers.

There is a conscious decision to be made by leaders and their colleagues about what time they intend to give formally and informally to these legitimate constituents and how collectively they intend to discharge it. The judgement of how far another member of the team will go as the corporate representative at a particular meeting is crucial: it will vary from time to time, as well as the occasions on which more than one of the team is involved. We will elaborate shortly on how successful heads use their time. In the meantime, let's examine some of the secrets of using that time well.

There are two aspects. First, those in time as it affects organization (the timetable, the pattern of meetings, the rhythm of the school year), and second as it affects the individual participant.

We have already implied the importance of the choice of the representative at particular meetings in the approach to time management. We always admired the headteachers who sometimes sent a deputy to a local authority briefing meeting as much as we did those who, on occasions, came with their deputy. If the same head deployed both strategies we were pretty confident that at least we were in the presence of someone who had thought through the issue of time.

We also admired the principal who would arrange to meet a difficult parent, not in his own study but in the year-head's room, thereby subtly implying that the year-head and not the principal was the person who settled the issue in question. The same principal would retreat from such a meeting as the coffee arrived with, 'Well look, you two seem to be sorting it out . . . I know you will forgive me Mrs Smith if I just leave you to finish it off. It has been good to see you, don't hesitate to let us [with a gesture to the year-head] know if we can help on a future occasion.'

If a head is always accessible, it is almost as bad as never being seen. It really is a subtle issue. Increasingly one hears that the heads are outside school more than they are in it. It is a danger sign if that is perceived to be the case, although as the person expected to be the interpreter of the organization to the external interest groups and so many other legitimate bodies, some time away from school is inevitable, especially at a time of great change. The orchestra will continue to play without a conductor – for a while.

Local authorities need to be careful not to conspire unwittingly in disabling headteachers by making too frequent calls on their time: they need particularly to counsel those heads who always appear to be a 'representative' of their fellows because they may be exhibiting signs of goal displacement. They may be running out of creative steam within their schools. We will return to this later.

'It's all very well to look at Belbin and Myers Briggs', a colleague remarked ominously one day, 'but I think the infant teacher could teach us a thing or two about what to look for in a leadership team. After all, she assesses her charges' progress in listening, speaking, reading and writing, and while they are doing it, she looks to see whether they are thinking and learning. If we could get that right in our team', she concluded with a smile, 'we would be doing all right.'

She was referring to our practice of putting every new member of staff through the Myers–Briggs profile of preferred leadership operational styles, and then inviting an external coach to talk to us about ways in which we could improve our collective efforts. Nothing too unusual in that: most school leadership teams do something similar. They use coaches, assess the profile of preferred operational styles of leadership and work at the gaps. They rotate chairing of meetings and encourage departments to do the same. It's standard practice.

The more we thought about our colleague's remarks the more sense they made and we realized how easy it was to neglect one or the other of the four activities of listening, speaking, reading and writing. It certainly provides a very useful compass in looking at how successful headteachers spend their time.

Think about it. First, there's the obvious point about the much misunderstood phrase 'time to think'. As one head dismissively told me: 'I do my thinking all the time. It occupies every waking moment. When I want to focus the sum total of my thinking, I spend an evening writing or', he added, 'speak with a group of colleagues. Out of that comes my own or our collective refreshed direction or the solution to a problem.'

Second, if you analyse what you do each day, it can be broken down into 'listening, speaking, reading and writing'. Most forms of human activity, apart from sleeping, usually involve one or more of these four.

Third – and this is surely the key for the successful headteacher – you can only read and write in isolation, whereas you need people to listen and talk. That's presumably why another successful head said to me forcefully: 'I never look at my computer – the email or whatever – between eight in the morning and half-past five in the evening. Nor do I do any paperwork then either. I can do all of that before and afterwards, because I do that alone. The time the school's in session is precious. The whole community is there. And it's therefore time for the pupils, the staff, governors and other members of the wider community.'

She went on to say that if she ever found herself inadvertently backing away from that guiding principle and staying in her office, she knew she was on a very slippery slope.

Time is so precious that some people say that learning to use time wisely and to best effect is the key skill for a headteacher to master. That's why the 'listening, speaking, reading and writing' overlay on the use of a head's time is so useful – it helps them to guard against wasting time by being alone during the school day. Indeed, it has led more than one head we know to share an office with deputies, so that when they are in the same place together, they are also sharing ideas (or for that matter agreeing) an approach to a difficult immediate issue. They claim there's never a problem about a room to themselves for a private meeting.

> **Schools are places where there can never be too much of the senior team being around and lending a hand.**

To conclude this section on the use of precious time we have attempted to describe five main uses to which successful school leaders devote their time.

First use of time

They are 'skalds' not 'scolds'.

The word 'skald' is reserved in Scandinavian folklore for the poets who told stories to warriors before battle. The stories were always positive and reminded people of past great deeds, as well as impending future triumphs. In our culture, Shakespeare's construction of Henry V's speech before Agincourt is an equivalence. It's the same with heads. There is a touch of the 'skaldik' about all the successful ones. They use awards days to reflect out loud that: 'Last summer's results at GCSE were the best ever, however you look at them. But this year's Year 11, who are with us tonight, are the best year group we have ever had, so we know that next summer will be better still. And when I look at last summer's Key Stage 3 results and talk with the head of Year 10 we know this trend will continue.'

> The art of the headteacher, as skald or storyteller, encompasses imagery, metaphor, simile, analogy and an unerring sense of timing and occasion.
>
> Tim Brighouse (2007)

Assemblies are the same, with tales of sporting and other success achieved and impending. Staff briefings are occasions to tell of the brilliant way a member of staff dealt with a pupil in the corridor and followed by a low-key apology for mentioning it 'because I know it's something that all of you do . . . but I was just reminded of the quality of our staff when I saw it.'

Key opportunities for being skaldik

Assemblies, staff meetings, parents' evenings, concerts, plays and major occasions are all key opportunities not to be easily passed up. Outside the school, too, the canny head repeats some of the best stories as, in an accumulating received wisdom, do other members of staff. They know that the perception of more good things than bad things happening is one of the vital factors in school success.

The good outweighs the bad. The dictionary definition of 'scold' is 'to use undignified vehemence or persistence in reproof or fault-finding'. It is a quick and certain way to loose goodwill to emphasize the negative on public occasions. That way failure is at your elbow in no time at all. Yet heads can so easily fall victim to the habit. They are stretched and pulled every which way and, of course, they are often dealing with crisis or instances when 'singing from the same song-sheet' has become discordant or totally ignored. That's the time to remember that more good than bad things are happening, or if they are not that a positive 'can do' spirit will ensure they do. In *Essential Pieces: The jigsaw of a successful school* (2006), we referred to the need to overbalance heavily in favour of what we described as 'appreciative enquiry', that is finding what is good in 'what is'. If the head isn't an energy-creator in their interactions, then nobody else can fully compensate.

Being a *skald* probably takes up three/four hours each week . . . and not being a 'scold' a lot longer! It should not be confused with talking that happens all the time – but it does embrace both speaking to large and small groups and telling stories.

Second use of time

They sit on the wall, not the fence.

The morning is important in any organization and perhaps nowhere more so than in schools, where the teacher's every move can affect a student's disposition to learn. You have a personal crisis? The shopping needs to be done? Despite all this, the good teacher forces herself to find time to greet colleagues and students cheerfully in the walk from the bus stop or car park to the school buildings. She knows that how she is with her class or tutor group is going to influence the day for many of her students. So avoiding a pre-occupied, or worse still a grumpy or even hostile, appearance is a priority for the teacher.

It's no different with heads.

> The morning habit of many a primary headteacher was to sit on the wall or stand at the school gate, where he could be seen having a cheery word with all and sundry as they ran into school.
>
> 'It's the chance for parents to nobble me too, and', he added reflectively, 'how the majority do that helps to set the tone for the awkward few parents, who otherwise could storm into school to vent their own frustration with life on me. Either I or the deputy does the same at the end of the day too.'

A successful south London secondary head in a large school does something similar when he stands everyday in the entrance foyer for half an hour from about a quarter-past eight, so that entering staff can buttonhole him and ask for a word later in the day. As the head says, 'I'll always make sure that I get back to them the same day. It's my interpretation of an 'open door' practice, because I am never in my office except for meetings.'

Another headteacher can be seen on the City Road in Birmingham of an afternoon supervising bus queues and waving to parents in cars picking up their children. Such heads are deeply conscious of their need to be accessible to all the school community, if not at once, at least at some point during the day. The head knows only too well that the less time spent in the office the better.

The school walk

In the same spirit, therefore, of being accessible, the practice of the 'daily school walk' is key. It means visiting all (and not avoiding some) phase or faculty areas, talking with kitchen or catering staff and having a word with cleaners, as well as all the other school staff – learning mentors, teaching assistants, ground staff and the back-up administrative staff – who comprise the management engine of the school. When using the word 'daily' we are not implying that all of these 'people interactions' happen every day, but that time is built in, so that they do happen with planned regularity. Another successful head has devised a variant on this, by engaging in 'pupil-tracking' – that is accompanying a couple of pupils throughout a school day – at least once a term. 'You can learn a lot in a day about what is worrying kids – and, of course, it reduces the need to do as much formal monitoring of lessons that way.'

'Sitting on the wall' also symbolizes the need for the head to be at the edge of the organization – that is, the main conduit to the world beyond the school. Lunchtime patrols of the local community, the shops and the streets enable the head and leadership colleagues to take the pulse of what is happening, as well as visit fellow workers in the local health clinic, neighbourhood office or advice bureau.

'Not sitting on the fence' is a caution not to equivocate or procrastinate too often. Schools are places where people are quick to detect whether a delay to give due consideration to a difficult issue or to secure consensus about something is genuine, or merely a device to conceal a head's lack of moral backbone and failure to be consistent. It's as well not to dwell too much on the negative, so it's probably not sensible to provide examples. All of us can bring them to mind.

However, the head who becomes 'invisible' to the community, by spending too much time in the office or outside the school, is in danger of not sitting on the wall often enough and thereby forfeiting the confidence of staff. Sitting on the wall in its many manifestations – school walks, lunchtime tours of the local area, pupil pursuits – can take up to 30 hours a week.

Third use of time

They teach, learn and assess for most of their time.

The PriceWaterhouseCoopers study into school leadership (2007) envisages a time when principals of schools or groups of schools will not have had teaching experience. That seems to us an improbable recipe for success: after all, even education officers in local authorities were expected to have done some teaching. Certainly, it's the perception of those heads who have been very successful – and their staff – that part of their credibility comes from their expert interest in teaching and, of course, from learning and assessment. 'If I'm not seen as a reasonable practitioner, I'm simply not credible in the staffroom', is how one head put it, as we reflected on the desirability of being seen to do playground duty or take over the teaching of a Year 9 class on a Friday afternoon. There are many ways of demonstrating their interest in teaching.

Regular teaching?

How they demonstrate their teaching is a different matter. Probably it's not sensible for the head to have a regular teaching slot. (Mind you: ask any head of a two- or three-teacher primary school and while they might agree, they will comment that 'chance would be a fine thing!') In a large school, however, apart from anything else, the head will get dragged away too often to be fair to the students. Of course, school assemblies need to be stunningly brilliant occasions in the very successful school and the head must be seen as a good performer and to take her part in circulating to every tutor group, where there is a difficult issue to talk through with students and where the intimacy of the tutor group is the right place to do it.

Our preference for how to demonstrate an interest and competence in teaching lies with the example of the head who, with her deputies, earmarked three Tuesdays and Wednesdays each term and 'gave' them in rotation to faculties. Members of staff could pursue lesson observations, either within the school or in visits to comparable schools with known interesting practice. As the head observed, it had the added benefit of enabling the leadership team to compare notes and discuss issues afterwards so that faculty reviews were better informed. Another always does a short course with Year 7 in order 'that I can get to know their names quickly and ensure they know the "legacy" of the school that they are inheriting and to which, in due course, they will contribute'.

Teaching adults as well as pupils

Teaching pupils is one thing, teaching adults another. Yet like the good teacher the successful headteacher, by the use of 'appreciative enquiry', is an excellent coach. Conversations with staff seek to identify what's good in their practice and how it might be extended, by supporting the member of staff's assumed ambition for excellence. They facilitate visits and show interest in the outcomes. They encourage teachers to have videos of their own practice. They celebrate the faculty, which has created a bank of videoed key lessons, so that students who miss lessons – or understanding the point at the time – can refer to them later. In their teaching, they know that they have to model excellent explanation and story-telling and high-quality questioning. Indeed, it's worth adding as an aside that they are better at asking the right questions than in hurrying to provide answers, tempting though it is to do so.

But 'questioning' raises the issue of the heads themselves providing an example of being a learner. Respecting the expert knowledge of the subject specialist is the obvious everyday way of doing so. It's the head's job to bring all this expert knowledge together so, coupled with their own greater understanding of what is happening beyond the school, they can make a greater sense of the whole. In that sense they are what Michael Fullan has called 'knowledge creators'. They may even have a research project of their own and they certainly encourage further study among their staff. They find articles to share with individual staff. They rotate the role of 'chair' in meetings of the senior team and encourage faculty leaders to do the same. Informally, they ask speculative and genuinely enquiring questions and formally they may even have a shared 'learning-plan' for the year. Their interest in assessment shows not merely in their regular 360° feedback exercises but in their often demonstrated commitment to improving on their own previous best. They are interested in the changes in external assessments and, of course, keep abreast of Ofsted changes in inspection practices. It's worth commenting here that a recent Ofsted inspection of a London secondary school rested almost entirely on the HMI observing a head's observation and debrief of a randomly chosen member of staff's lesson! So successful heads practise 'formative' assessment for staff and are active in the review of pupils' progress, which is at the heart of 'assessment for learning'.

These activities can take up anything from two to ten hours in a week.

Fourth use of time

They spend their evenings, weekends and holidays . . . working . . . socializing and being members of a family.

If reading and writing are best done alone, it follows that they will happen outside school days and terms. The arrival of email is a sore test of that. Add to that the avalanche of promised change in paper form and through website access, and it means that any head needs some system to keep on top of the task of 'seeing wider and further', while dealing with the sheer volume of day-to-day business.

That's why one head, who has claimed never to use her computer during school hours, explains how she makes it happen. She has an agreement with her PA and office manager to spend 15 minutes each morning after they are first in, with an equivalent session each evening, picking up her folder of items and post. The post that they have sifted is dealt with either at home or before everyone arrives the next morning. 'My selected emails are marked as unread and the urgent ones in red and I deal with them on my laptop out of school hours.'

However, that does mean that successful heads get up and arrive early and leave to go to bed late. They know that those are the times when they wrestle with the strategic and with downright boring or painful chores. Intricate personal, legal and budgetary matters can be incredibly time-consuming. Judicious and skilled delegation will take you so far and needs to be mastered. Indeed, in many matters of appeal, they are essential and, in the end, there's no avoiding a lot of apparently unproductive time. Governors' meetings are outside school time, as are the many school sporting fixtures, musical events and celebratory occasions. As one head, who had overcome a lifetime's lack of interest in sport, put it: 'Showing interest in something I was not originally or naturally much interested in is one of the first unexpected things which I discovered in headship.'

It's in the evenings (well, those that are free of school engagements) after watching television with their families that heads read articles, or alternatively in the early mornings, before the rest of the house is awake.

Eating, either at working breakfasts or in restaurants in the evening, can often also be part of the rhythm of the heads of larger schools. Taking on the tradition of the nineteenth-century legends like Arnold, their families will sometimes be ensnared in school-related activity. Neither are some parts of the holiday sacrosanct. One successful head spent at least half her three weeks in France last summer putting together a very impressive 'So you want one day to be a head?' course, which she then ran for 17 volunteers from the staff on Friday afternoons.

Time outside school on these sorts of task will vary widely. Sometimes it's very heavy, at others it's blissfully peaceful.

Fifth use of time

They spend two hours a week in acts of unexpected kindness.
One of the most overlooked aspects of successful leadership involves what might be called the 'personal touch' – not just remembering people's personal concerns but in acts of unexpected kindness. Before examining these in particular, it's perhaps worth noting that the present concern with 'personalization' must involve the modelling of it from the head. Unless you know people, you are lost. It's why it's much more difficult to be a successful head in your early days, when you don't know people.

That's also why those destined to be successful heads spend the months before taking up appointment with photos and the personal files of staff, so that when they arrive they have a flying start. We know one head who took this to the lengths of looking at the photos of Year 7 and Year 9 pupils, 'since they are the ones who, when I arrive, are going to make the most difference to how my early influence on the school is perceived'. One may disagree with her selection or even her motivation, but it is hard to fault her reasoning, intentions or commitment.

Feeling special

This last and most important element of 'expenditure of time' derives from a head's commitment to people and realizing that everyone needs to feel special. Hence, birthdays are remembered and emergencies in staff private lives catered for. Privacy is respected, so the handwritten note or the word in the corridor expressing thanks for some small contribution made by a member of staff provide the energy that sustains collective spirit. One head told us she keeps lots of cards for birthdays and other events and doesn't leave on Fridays without sitting down and reviewing the week. Even an email will sometimes do! Most successful heads confess to practise like this and most will say that, however spontaneous it may seem to recipients, it requires a system – not least in order to avoid the impression that there are 'favourites' and 'outcasts'.

Leadership – the main tasks

So, if those are the five main definitions of expenditure of headteacherly time, and if we have set out earlier the skills of 'delegation' and 'managing change', what are the leader's main tasks? We think there are six.

1   *They create energy:*
Their own example – what they say, what they believe, who they are – is one of indomitable will and a passion for success that is at once courageous and brooks no denial. They talk not about staff but with staff. They ask 'what if' speculative questions. They are fussy about appointments, taking care not to make permanent appointments of 'energy-consumers'. Because they are full of hope they look for optimists – those who say 'how we could' rather than 'why we can't'. They show interest in every aspect of school life.

2   *They build capacity:*
Again, they set an example. They teach themselves and are observed by staff doing so, or they take over a class to let others observe somebody else's practice. They rotate the chairing of meetings to develop the skill of others. They ensure that young staff members are involved in a 'school improvement group' and act on their suggestions. They have a programme for staff development that considers the better future of the individual, as well as of the school. They know and cherish all the interests of all staff, especially those that the staff had in previous jobs or still have in the world beyond school. They use the collective first-person pronoun 'we' rather than the singular 'I'. They take the blame when it's not their fault and they are generous with praise to others for collective success. They set an example of learning, for instance by adopting an annual learning-plan. They read and share articles and encourage others to do the same.

3   *They meet and minimize crisis:*
At a time of genuine crisis they find cause for optimism and hope, for points of learning. They stay calm. They acknowledge their own mistakes. They are 'pogo-stick' players in the sense that they can simultaneously be in the thick of things, as it were, yet still be seeing the wider picture.

A present crisis is the source for vital learning and future improvement. They themselves show willing to be a 'utility player' – one who, *in extremis*, will turn their hand to any task.

4 *They secure and enhance the environment:*
They ensure classroom teaching and learning materials are well organized and in plentiful supply. They make sure the management arrangements are seen by staff as 'fit for purpose' – right in detail and serving the needs of both staff and students alike. For example, they often review meetings to ensure that 'transactional' or 'business' meetings are minimized. The staff handbook is repeatedly updated and the computer system works and provides a useful database for staff, all of whom have laptops, and for students who, with parents, have access at school and remotely to lesson plans, to homework tasks, to reports and to progress grades. They improve the staffroom and the whole environment of school – both visually and aurally.

5 *They seek and chart improvement:*
They use comparative benchmarking data both within school and from other schools. They are keen on 'benchmarking', but they do so in a climate of encouraging risk. They themselves ensure there is a proper mix of 'appreciative enquiry' and problem-solving. Appreciative enquiry involves finding and celebrating what's good and engaging in a search for what's outstanding – by visiting other practitioners and finding out what research tells us before deciding on a plan of action to deliver excellence. This is a process of 'energy-creation'. Problem-solving, on the other hand, concerns staff with barriers and problems that have cropped up. They require analysis and the creation of possible solutions before deciding on a plan of action. This is a frequently necessary process, but it consumes energy, more in some people than in others. Therefore the successful leader, conscious of this, seeks to create a climate of much appreciation when solving problems.

Those who seek and chart improvement celebrate genuine (and it must be genuine) success. They know the best of 'genuine' is an improvement on past practice, whether individual or collective. However, they celebrate other social events too, in order to create the climate in which energy, capacity and ultimate success depend. Governors' meetings and staff meetings, awards ceremonies and 'briefings' are crucial to that. They are, above all, good at 'collective' as opposed to 'individual' monitoring.

6 *They are always extending the vision of what's possible:*
Clearly, this involves being both historian and futurologist. Any leader wishing to extend the vision of what's possible is deeply aware of this double requirement, especially since the present dominates so much of school life. If sometimes that present seems overwhelming, the energy levels drop. Telling stories that remind people of past success and that honour successful predecessors and the school's history is a thing wise leaders do. However, they are also forecasters of the weather and describers of future possibilities. They confidently describe a path from the present to the future. They are good listeners and readers. They write 'future' pieces for their community. They ask 'why not' aloud and 'why' silently in their heads.

These qualities apply to all levels of leadership, from the class teacher with her pupils up to the head. For much of her time the class teacher marches to the rhythm of the timetable and the lesson bell. Not so the headteacher.

We have written so much of this chapter with an illustrative bias towards heads, but there are similar considerations for the deputies and assistant heads, for the heads of faculties or years . . . indeed for anyone with a leadership responsibility in the school. As we explain elsewhere, we think it applies to every member of staff in a truly successful school.

Stages of leadership

Again, we illustrate the eternal dilemma of the leader – about knowing how to start well, how not to go stale and get a second wind, and above all how to leave without undoing all the good you have achieved – with the head in mind, but again the issues apply to anyone with a leadership role.

- *Stage 1: Initiation*

  First is the 'initiation' stage. The newcomer is trying to establish, with each and every one of their stakeholder groups, that 'what they say', 'what they do' and 'who they are' match up. People always want early proof about the first two – and none more so than pupils and staff, who have finely tuned antennae for the bogus or the uncertain of purpose.

  Increasingly nowadays there are other important stakeholders that new heads need to persuade of their trustworthiness, not least governors, parents and the wider community interests. Initial contacts are crucial . . . the first staff meeting, the assembly and the tone of the introductory letter to parents. For the deputy promoted internally there are other challenges – not least proving that you can carry off the subtly different role with colleagues who knew you as deputy. Despite the differences, the process is the same. The 'initiation' stage will last for different times with different stakeholder groups, although each will be telling others of their impressions.

  Tragically, some heads never get beyond the 'initiation' stage, because they don't establish themselves. That is the prelude for a very painful period, as their mismatch with the school they have joined becomes apparent to all. Some – thankfully few – people leave headship with a bitter taste in their mouth.

- *Stage 2: Development*

  Second is the 'developmental' stage: when the head is known and when the defining nature of the head's chapter can proceed with certainty of sufficient support to have a fair chance of carrying it to a successful outcome.

  All stages of headship have their hazards but none more so than the third. The first five to seven years have seen the completion of the initial aims; a plateau is reached where there is the need to take stock and pause to draw breath.

- *Stage 3: Stall*

    Here, then, is the risk of the 'stall' – where it's all too tempting to think that you can allow the school to run on autopilot. Peter Mortimore *et al.*'s (1988) research evidence is that heads are at their best between the third and seventh years. That doesn't mean to say that they can't then change gear and start another developmental stage – indeed many do – simply that it's easy not to do so. In this third period bad habits can creep in. You may stop giving time within the school and can become preoccupied with matters outside.

- *Stage 4: Decline*

    Finally, there is the 'decline': you have announced you're leaving and the 'lame duck' period beckons. It is best to make this short, rather than telegraph it over a long period.

Some final questions

Of themselves and their beliefs:

1 How aware of my beliefs or value systems are the staff for whom I am responsible?
   - Do they know them through papers written for staff meetings? By my comments at meetings? By what I say at assemblies?
   - Am I sure my actions in respect of staff, pupils and my use of time match those beliefs?
   - What actions in the last week, month, term, prove that I value individual members of staff?

2 How far do the institution's practices, marking, awards evenings, procedures for staff appointments, reflect our collective beliefs?
   - Of their personal skills and competencies and their match with the institution.

3 When we last appointed a member of the team, how did we analyse the complementary qualities we needed for a successful team?
   - Did we need someone strong in planning, organizing, maintaining, monitoring or evaluating?
   - Did we need, for example, one whose strengths were in shaping or finishing?

4 How do I use my team and other members of the team to the best match of their own strengths and to the task we need to perform collectively?

5 How are the persons assigned particular responsibilities and tasks briefed? Are they asked to reflect on the processes they will be required to implement in order to bring the task to a successful conclusion or is it just left to chance?

Of the processes within the institution:

6 Do those with leadership roles (whether in the senior team departmentally or at main-grade level) receive training appropriate to their expected role, for example in chairing meetings, in being coordinators, in producing reports, in establishing monitoring systems, in writing letters to parents?

7 How far can opportunities for leadership be extended?

Of time and tasks:

8 How do I ensure that I allocate time to those who need praise and reassurance or

interest in what they do for the school? How much time am I spending outside the school? Does my time commitment match the priority tasks of the school?

9 Am I visible to staff, parents and pupils and am I seen in tasks/activities that reinforce the common purpose and values we collectively wish to promote within the school?

Ten points for leaders to remember and help to preserve their sanity

Whether as a head of department, a main-grade teacher with leadership responsibility for a particular aspect of school life or as a headteacher, there are a few simple dos and don'ts. The best list we came across was in Canada, prepared by a teachers' federation in conjunction with Professor Michael Fullan of the University of Toronto. He had ten points. We are not so ambitious and will settle for eight of his and two of our own. Our first for crucial work–life balance and helps to counteract our own tendency to be workaholics!

1 *Manage your diary*
   There is little chance of surviving – let alone being successful – as head with all these competing demands made upon you without diary management. This can be achieved in more than one way. To those new to headship it may be a new experience if, as is often the case, the lesson bell and timetable have dictated the use of time for you.
   Whatever method chosen, the role of the PA is vital. She or he must know your every move. Whether you carry your own diary or deliberately don't (and both seem legitimate methods if the views and practices of successful heads are accepted) the PA must have the master copy, so she can protect your time. In order to survive, most experienced heads build into their diaries 'down time' when they can choose what in their judgement they need to do to. In doing so, they stop themselves becoming prisoners of events. Such practice requires a code shared with the PA, so that others don't look over her shoulder and see a blank space which they think they can fill.
   Build 'lungs' of time into your diary once a fortnight. Make sure that every half-term you use one of these lungs to go off site and talk with another friend or acquaintance doing a similar job.

2 *Have a 7–10 year service!*
   After 7–10 years either:
   • Have a half-term or term off with the purpose of coming back refreshed, seeing the school with new eyes and setting off on another chapter of development or;
   • Leave and move on, perhaps to a second or third headship, when you can start all over again with not such an impossibly extended stakeholder group. (After all, there will be the chance to build that up gradually.)

3   *Keep it simple.*

So many of us overelaborate. One teacher I knew overplanned and overmanaged so that everyone felt oppressed by long documents, complex diagrams and elaborate systems that logically should have worked well if only they had not been surrounded by human beings with all the frailty of memory, misunderstanding and fallibility we all bring to our daily lives. The more elaborate the planning and management, the more likely it is that things will go wrong. The Canadians put it nicely when they say that 'striving for complexity in the absence of action can generate more clutter than clarity'.

Moreover the real sense of camaraderie and ownership always comes from shared action rather than shared planning. If you intend to have a grand vision it's best to get started in a small way with a few things. The more complex the change, the more important it is that the planning and managing is loose: for to tackle it otherwise encourages dependency and diminishes the improvisation essential at the start of any important changing enterprise.

4   *Avoid transferring the blame to actions beyond your control*

Colleagues are often inclined to sympathize with leaders as having an impossible job. Such notions must be rigorously resisted and leaders must give the impression that anything is possible if the group are determined to do it. 'If only . . . ' is an excuse not to address an issue. It renders people powerless and inactive. The Education Act of 1988 is a reality, as is the shortage of cash and the teacher shortage or the teacher surplus. The children from the estate do come from such backgrounds and their expectations to become committed competent adults and citizens have to be raised. Leaders must convey that everything is not merely possible but likely. If we waste time lamenting the local authority's lack of direction, the parents' fecklessness, the government's neglect or malign intent we become paralysed, reinforce dependence and waste time in our need to give urgent attention to raising the aspirations and achievements in the next generation.

5   *Concentrate on important issues like curriculum and teaching that also reinforce the professional culture of the school*

Teachers nowadays say that they would enjoy their job more if there were only more time for teaching. That reflects not only their proper sense of priority but the way in which so many of the priorities signalled from outside seem to have little or nothing to do with their main purpose, that of teaching and learning with the children. One of the heads I most respect argues that curriculum change is what teachers respond to most. 'Put them in teams and the outcome is magical' is how she described it. If you do concentrate on a few things, make them as closely related to teaching and learning as possible. As for their culture, ask questions about how the conversation and surroundings of the staffroom are to be made intellectually more stimulating as well as social.

6   *Practise being brave*

If their leaders can back the decision to concentrate on a few things by publicly deciding to pass some new opportunities by, or better still to negotiate a later date for the completion of a directive, the staff will feel empowered towards their common goal. If they see the leader take risks, they too will be more likely to be innovative, strong-minded and clearly focused. Some of the most outstanding headteachers I have known have been very angular to the local authority.

Good leaders sometimes have to take an independent stance on a matter of great public importance, and they are respected for it. Nor need courage be a negative matter: it is best exercised when it is cheerful, determined, positive and definite.

7 *Empower others*

An acid test of leaders occurs when something is revealed to be happening that is different, indeed rather daring or even risky, but not known to them. Of course their hearts miss a beat at such moments because they are being put at risk. But the best will not say, 'What on earth is happening?' but 'Isn't that great. How tremendous that such exciting things take place here. I must try harder to notice and congratulate good practice.' Staff need room and permission to try things out. They need also celebratory occasions for their successes.

8 *Build visions*

Not only you need to have a vision. Those on the staff trying out anything new can be encouraged to articulate their dreams of how it will be when the dream is realized in three years' time, or however long it takes to bring it to fruition. The consistent use of the word 'why?' can usually prod even the least forthcoming to reveal their dreams for the sometimes small changes they are trying to implement. From building on such small changes and visions, a department and a school can create an even larger shared vision.

9 *Decide what not to do and stop doing one of your regular tasks for a term to allow someone else to do it*

So many leaders burn themselves out by trying to do everything themselves, and so many more become impotent because they do nothing themselves. The issue of time-management is crucial. It is not 'doing things right' but 'doing the right things', as the cliché goes. We are certain that a leader is a public and not a private person, that it is the public occasions that take the time. Nevertheless, there is the necessity to decide what you are not doing and remember that one rule of management is that time must be used twice. Giving other people the chance to do part of the job contributes powerfully to 'succession planning'.

10 *Find some allies*

Interdependence is crucial for the stimulation of intellectual curiosity and the sharing of ideas. Other leaders in the system and other departmental groups outside the school are crucial, not least in ensuring that innovatory practices that you wish to espouse cannot be picked off as rogue and singular. The most exciting innovations are always being represented as part of mainstream thinking.

2 Organizing and delivering success

Efficiency is concerned with doing things right. Effectiveness is doing the right things.

Peter Drucker (1993)

Good schools face outwards as well as inwards, keeping their eye on the horizon as well as the bottom line.

David Hargreaves (1998)

If you do not raise your eyes you will think you are at the highest point.

Antonia Porchia

The need for organization

How well the school is organized and maintained (i.e. the administration and management of the school) vitally affects the lives of all who work and learn there. Poor organization and management is hugely debilitating, constantly sapping energy and motivation. By contrast, a school that has really thought through in detail the organization, providing and maintaining aspects of management, has established the foundations for success. In a sense all this is obvious, but how often do schools attempt to address the urgent priorities facing them without considering the detail of resource management and organization? Such are the pressures that it is tempting to tackle the areas needing action head on without dealing thoroughly with the administrative and organizational barriers to success.

We sometime overhear conversations from parents and members of the wider community that their own school is 'a well-run school'. They don't necessarily mean that their school is an outstanding school in Ofsted terms but that from their various standpoints the school does the following well:

- Communicates effectively through *personal* letters, emails, mobile phone technology, newsletters, calendar of activities and key dates.
- Organizes efficiently all meetings with parents, particularly those meetings where parents, pupils and teachers can review progress and plan what needs to be done to succeed in the future.
- Consistently applies the homework policy and involves parents in ensuring that this happens.
- Organizes community events that involve local shops, businesses, community centres, residents' accommodation and places of worship.
- Follows up letters and telephone calls as promptly and efficiently as any business practising 'customer care' and greets and treats visitors courteously and efficiently.

Organisations only work well where there is a common belief in what you're trying to achieve.

Greg Dyke

School staff will also have a view on how well the school is run (although they of course have their part to play) and if there are constant snags in the administration, it is almost impossible to counter staff stress and loss of morale. Good schools are rigorous in consistently applying exacting standards at all times and at all levels. Good communications, thorough collaborative planning and a high level of consistent application of school policies, are essential to the organization and delivery of success and there are some essential ingredients that will allow this to happen.

The staff handbook

The staff handbook is at the heart of the school's smooth operation. Time and again, schools that run into difficulty realize too late that they've allowed their staff handbook to fall into neglect and therefore be overlooked. From the smallest to the largest school, the handbook needs to be well organized, quickly accessible and always kept up to date. Although good handbooks might vary, they all include the school's plans, policies and practices – at their best a simple A4 sheet for each policy and practice and kept in loose-leaf form. On this sheet there will be a brief statement of both policy and the implications for practice, with the name of the member of staff with overall responsibility for its application and for leading the next review of policy and practice, and the date on which it is to be reviewed (thereby reaffirming the principle of continuous review referred to earlier). There are also the names of the teams of people responsible for implementing different aspects of the practice. When there is any change, and this is inevitable, the revised version is formally included as an item of information at a staff briefing and the replacement sheet inserted in all copies. Usually there are copies in the staffroom, different areas of the school and the school office, although of course each member of staff has their own. The best schools now have their staff handbook in electronic form and readily available to all through their e-learning platform.

Job-descriptions

Crucially job-descriptions will relate to the staff handbook in the sense that the description of 'lead' and 'support' responsibilities for different aspects of school life will be reflected in the tasks necessary to carry out the policies. The best schools now avoid a long list of duties ending with the catch-all 'and such other duties as may from time to time be determined', preferring instead to list 'lead' responsibilities along with 'support' responsibilities, the latter usually in teams. Job-descriptions are also closely linked to 'performance management' or 'professional development' (whatever language to describe these is thought appropriate). In the best schools job-descriptions are always subject to review and change. In this way leadership at all levels can be reviewed and rotated to the benefit of the individual and the school as a whole (see Chapter 4 for the detail on job-descriptions).

Staff induction

The underlying policy and the details of the practices will be included in the staff handbook, but induction is worth picking out because it is a vital support to maintaining consistency, especially where there is high staff turnover. Staff induction must encompass all staff, teaching and support alike. It should contain a common element for all within a set programme. Normally the programme will be organized on an annual cycle and it will offer opportunities for those who arrive at the beginning of the school year, or during it, to have a brief, repeated general introduction. The induction programme will be carefully structured and focused, particularly on what the school knows are the vital elements in 'singing from the same song-sheet' and integrated into general professional development.

Calendars and communications

These are important both internally and externally as previously referred to, but an agreed calendar of events that all staff see and negotiate before putting in new entries and that avoids clashes and potential recrimination, is a basic building-block of a good school. Again, in the best schools, this is now in electronic form readily available to all for consultation.

'The way we do things round here' – living the values and beliefs

Schools often have a different reality or mindset of school life and their own mindset in relation to what occurs in their external environment. This is because their culture is shaped by their history, context and the people in it, particularly leaders. Good and successful schools will have an explicit culture and ethos with clear values, beliefs and purposes enabling them to articulate a unique identity and share these with newcomers, whether staff, pupils or parents. This will manifest itself in customs, rituals, symbols, stories and language. Thus pupils' learning, achievements or discipline are emphasized constantly in assemblies or other collective occasions framed by high expectations. In terms of professional relationships there is a culture of staff choosing to work together, to share ideas and practices, and a belief in continuous improvement.

The whole-school community maintains positive relationships and social cohesion through continued instances of courtesy, respect and reinforcing accepted norms of behaviour, despite different and competing subcultures often based on gender, race, language, ethnicity and socioeconomic status.

> Change is the sum of a thousand acts of reperception and behaviour at every level of the organisation.
>
> John Kao (1996)

Good schools recognize that they are always in the business of strengthening their culture and ethos but that this can mean being open to 're-culturing' – the process of developing new values, beliefs and norms.

Workforce reform

Good organization sets the foundations for the delivery of success, but it is the school workforce that will ensure the delivery of success through getting the best outcomes for learners. Workforce remodelling has enabled schools to draw a line under a divided past. There was an 'upstairs' and 'downstairs' mentality in many schools, which implied that there were two sorts of staff – 'teachers' and 'non-teachers' – despite an uncomfortable awareness that the most powerful people in the school were often the school secretary and the school caretaker!

The introduction of workforce remodelling and the TLRs or TLAs (Teaching and Learning Responsibilities or Teaching and Learning Allowances) has forced schools to rethink who does what and set it out in appropriate job-descriptions. In the best schools there has been thoughtful inclusion of 'whole-school' responsibilities that straddle the 'teacher' divide. Many schools now have their bursar as part of the senior management team and heads of year sometimes have a social care background rather than a teaching background, which is all the better to deliver the *Every Child Matters* agenda. Examinations administration and cover supervision have been remodelled. Good schools have been very creative and inclusive in appointing the best workforce to fit the context of the school, and getting the best out of that workforce in promoting achievement and higher standards. They are prepared to question why things are done in a given way and to pay a little to gain a lot. They manage staff by implementing policies and procedures to ensure effective recruitment, training and deployment.

They have chosen to re-culture the organization not just through the better use of time, space and buildings but crucially in roles and responsibilities. Over the last few years there has been a steady increase in the appointment of teaching and learning assistants, integration assistants and learning mentors to help schools personalize approaches to learning. However, increasingly this is being supplemented by the appointment of a whole range of coaches and mentors who can offer highly specialist support whether to gifted and talented pupils, those with special needs or those pupils willing to pursue a specialist interest such as sport, languages, music and the arts generally. Some of the best examples of workforce remodelling are to be found in using expert IT technicians to maximize teaching and learning opportunities (sometimes shared in primary schools), or staff with a school design/display/photography brief to help improve the learning environment. Good schools are making sure that their classrooms and learning areas are rich in the number of trained adults available to support learning to new high standards. Inevitably the process of personalization increases the rate of specialism so that the needs of pupils can be met better. As the workforce grows in numbers some of them will become increasingly specialized in knowledge, skills and functions.

Delivering success

We have talked elsewhere about the essential factors that make good and outstanding schools, and in particular leadership at all levels of the school, the drive constantly to improve teaching, learning and assessment and the importance of collective review and school self-evaluation in identifying the right provision for improvement. Yet further than this, the best schools are alive to the best interventions or levers that can make a difference at a pace. One of the features of these schools is that they are always looking for new and better ways of doing things.

> Success and its identification is like a fast-breeder reactor of energy fission.
>
> **Margaret Maden (2001)**

We have written previously about interventions and change processes in school improvement, most particularly in *How to Improve your School* (1999), but also in other publications since then. As we said at the beginning of this book, David Hargreaves has written convincingly about 'low-leverage' interventions where a lot of effort goes into a new practice or policy and the pay-off is paltry, and 'high-leverage' interventions taking relatively low effort to formulate or implement, but yielding extremely powerful outcomes in terms of learning and achievement.

Of course, we need to remind ourselves that in terms of interventions and levers context is crucial, with variables including the background of the students (race, socioeconomic, faith), the community the school serves (from affluent areas to those with considerable socioeconomic challenges) and where the school is in the local 'pecking-order', with consequences for admissions and budgets. In terms of school improvement too, every school is at a different point in the trajectory of its journey, but we are writing from the standpoint of what makes a good school now and we believe that all schools, either through critical self-evaluation or external consultancy, can identify those practices that can yield the highest leverage to help them become a good school, or if they are already good to maintain their success and become outstanding.

Despite the dangers of being too general in our prescriptions for delivering success or too detailed and explicit to fit certain contexts, we would like to suggest some key interventions that will make a difference to delivering success in addition to all that we have written in other sections of the book: that is about the processes and practices of school improvement.

We are of course referring to what we have called the 'butterfly effect'. What we now suggest is that schools make their own 'butterfly collection'.

Through this process the staff in the school continue to put into effect a number of small interventions that are capable of transforming behaviour, practice and culture. Most importantly, however, the staff are encouraged to engage continually in thinking, speculating and reflecting on the processes of school improvement and the subtleties of change. We believe that one of the characteristics of a good school is that they build collections of butterflies that make up a set of shared practice, which change behaviour at every level of the organization. Some schools are explicit about this, for example having a butterfly display, occasionally introducing butterflies in staff briefings or INSET opportunities, or producing their own collections. Others have different ways of capturing their examples of best practice and sharing them to make a difference. Good schools will make a judgement on those small levers or 'butterflies' that will make an individual and disproportionate difference to the further success of the school and systematize them across the organization.

> We need to prepare ourselves for the possibility that sometimes big changes follow from small events, and that sometimes these changes can happen very quickly.
>
> **Malcolm Gladwell (2000)**

The following figure describes the school butterfly effect diagrammatically, and sets out 12 examples of butterflies practised in schools.

Describe and define to the staff what butterflies are and how they can effect change.

↓

Design an appropriate pro forma to capture the essence of these small interventions, relating their effect to the seven processes of school improvement and their impact on changing practices.

↓

Initially ask all staff for three contributions that may affect teaching and learning practices.

↓

Publish these as a collection for dissemination and debate and decide on those to be collectively implemented.

↓

Build the collection of butterflies into the culture of the school by starting all staff meetings with the description of a butterfly, and asking for further contributions on specific themes such as raising achievement and promoting a positive ethos.

↓

Extend the process to include governors and the wider school community.

↓

Evaluate the cumulative effect of these many small interventions on the effectiveness of the school.

↓

Continue to publish and disseminate collections of new butterflies while reviewing, and if necessary modifying, those that are already being practised.

Figure 3 The school butterfly effect

Butterfly 1

'Singing from the same song-sheet': the seating-plan

Description

One school realized that consistency is crucial and also that new or weaker teachers are often 'tested' by pupils who are trying to establish whether they will stay for any length of time or are 'here today and gone tomorrow'. One of the time-honoured ways that some pupils do this is to try to sit where they want to. The school decided that ways of 'learning to work with a full range of fellow pupils' was to be a feature of their declared school policy. In the first week of each half-term therefore, at staff briefings, heads of year were asked to remind their year-group assemblies that in the following days they would be asked by each teacher to take their new seating positions. At each staff briefing for the following week colleagues were reminded so that everyone on the staff made a formality of establishing the seating-plan of each class they taught. In this way they claimed that weaker staff were not left so isolated.

Comment on impact

Deciding exactly where to draw the line in 'singing from the same song-sheet' is one of the most difficult questions for leadership teams. Get it too tight, with no room for individual freedom of teachers, and you lose creativity. Allow it to be too loose and the school's ethos in terms of pupils' behaviour suffers. The school that introduced this scheme discussed this every term in respect of many issues. It claims the 'seating-plan' theme is one they'll never change even though clearly experienced teachers know they don't need it.

Butterfly 2

Proximal learning

Description

The school agreed that it was more effective to have one whole-school focus for lesson observations undertaken by members of the middle and senior team. Structured talk in pairs or proximal learning was an early focus. Training on what made the proximal work effective was provided for all staff at a whole-school INSET. It was then agreed that every lesson, in every subject, for the term would have a slot for paired talk. All observations would only focus on proximal work so teachers could really get this right. For example, proximal work could form part of a starter or plenary session – talk together for two minutes on five effects of tropical storms you learned in the lesson – or a longer exercise, discussing a talk first and then completing a written element, often on a shared piece of paper. Giving a set amount of time for the proximal task is key. Students experienced this approach across the school and all soon became skilled at taking part.

Comment on impact

All students could do this. It worked powerfully as it was developing oral work across the whole school. Having one whole-school focus for observations ensured the initiative – small as it was – became quickly and very effectively embedded into the school. All staff now talk about 'putting some proximal into the lesson'. Staff share proximal activities that work particularly well. New staff observe lessons to see proximal work in action as it is such a key feature of the way staff teach. As a development it cost almost nothing and had a major impact. For boys (and reluctant writers) it enabled action first and writing second and it even gave weaker students things to say. Working in pairs and not small groups meant no student could 'hide' and opt out. All had to be engaged in the task. The quality of speaking skills improved very significantly in a very short time across the age, gender and ability range.

Butterfly 3

Subject teachers and their subject association

Description

Keeping up to date is a really difficult task in teaching, especially when there are so many national initiatives to learn about.

One secondary school decided that a priority had to be to encourage teachers to keep up their learning in their 'first love', that is their subject area. Each new member of staff would have their subject association (for example ASE, ATM/MA, MATE, HA and so on) membership paid for a year and the cost of attending the subject association's annual conference/meeting in their first year – along with a senior colleague.

Additionally they were given a £25 book-token to spend, and then had to present a review of the book at a faculty/departmental meeting.

Comment on impact

Both the initiatives were designed to support professional development and encourage new members of the profession to keep up to date with their subject. A variation on this was a school that subscribes to teachandlearn.net – the professional development service of the Open University that holds on its website current articles by leading thinkers in each subject area.

Butterfly 4

Work shadowing key posts in the school

Description

Ensuring that other colleagues develop some expertise in particular key areas in addition to that of the member of staff who has a designated responsibility for that area: for example cover, timetabling, school budgeting, examination procedures and administration. Areas in which this was already taking place would include work experience and certain pastoral positions.

Comment on impact

In addition to ensuring a smooth transition in the event of collision with the proverbial bus, this would give colleagues an additional experience to contribute to their career development. It would allow the sharing of ideas and benefit that always comes from having another point of view, thus developing a team approach. In time the 'shadow' may well take overall responsibility for that area and allow colleagues to move on to another area to develop a new expertise. In this way staff avoid becoming entrenched in one area, and new opportunities can be opened up as the cycle moves on.

This has implications for the way 'job-descriptions' are written. They are often long lists of tasks with the 'stomach-sinking' final one of 'such other duties as may . . . ' What this butterfly implants is a job-description where there are 'leading' or 'primary' responsibilities with 'secondary' or 'support' responsibilities.

Butterfly 5

Making walls talk

Description

Schools are always looking for easy ways to improve the environment. One school decided to find out the private interests and hobbies of all staff, using professional development and performance management interview and a review of application forms. Discovering a keen amateur photographer among the technicians, they commissioned her (for a £500 fee plus the cost of materials) to take an extensive and representative range of photographs of school activities – lessons, playtimes, sports workshops, drama, music, lunchtimes and staff meetings. They then paid £500 to another support staff colleague to mount and display the results throughout the school. The total cost of the scheme, including materials and so on, was £3,500, but the outcome was a much-appreciated exhibition of school and faculty life. The scheme is to be renewed each year.

A variation on this would be to get pupils with similar hobbies to run the schemes – again making sure they were suitably rewarded.

Comment on impact

The leadership team came up with this idea, but arranged for each faculty team to discuss it so that they could decide which area of display should be used, and whether the display could have a 'faculty' slant.

In exploring staff's private interest (in this instance photography), the school was keen to identify 'hyacinths' (see p. 90).

Butterfly 6

'Quid for a quote': a cost-effective way of improving the environment

Description

The headteacher believed that pieces of prose and poetry, as well as snappy epigrams and other quotations, are often an opportunity to stir the mind of the passer-by into profitable thought. He discussed his idea of 'quid for a quote' at a staff meeting. It was adopted enthusiastically.

At the start of the school year in each year assembly, the head of year and one of the school leadership team each presented a piece about one of their favourite quotations. This was followed up in the tutor group. The first homework of term was for each pupil in the school to go home and discuss with the family or carer five favourite quotes. On completion, at least one quote from each pupil was simply framed and displayed. The school then sent £1 home with the pupil for the parents to give to a charity of their choice.

Comment on impact

The visual, aural and behavioural environment of the school plays an important part in the likelihood of a school's success. Ensuring the visual environment is stimulating is always a problem. This scheme provided a simple way to raise awareness of the issue right across the school. (It is worth mentioning that the school in question is a 'rotting' 1960s/70s building, but internally is now a visual delight.)

Butterfly 7

Improving staff meetings:
sharing practice and collective review

Description

A primary school decided to hold its weekly staff meetings in classrooms rather than the staffroom or library. Every teacher would host a staff meeting on a rota basis and the first item on the agenda would be an explanation by the teacher of the particular learning environment and how the classroom was organized.

Comment on impact

Although somewhat apprehensive at first, teachers and learning assistants have found the process extremely useful in explaining and sharing ideas about classrooms and the organization of learning. This collective review process has helped teachers both to celebrate good practice and to improve on their previous best. The major topics that have been discussed concern classroom display, the organization of learning resources, the layout of the room and the development of particular learning areas. This process has led to the information of whole-school guidelines, a better appreciation of teaching and learning practice in the school and an improved quality of classroom organization and teaching.

Butterfly 8

Student supervisors

Description

The school already employed a range of teaching assistants and learning mentors. They decided also to recruit adults from the local community on a part-time basis, to act as student supervisors to patrol the school corridors, ensure pupils get to lessons punctually and are in lessons, and generally assist movement around the school. They wear distinctive red coats and now are a real part of the school community, valued by everybody.

Comment on impact

Although they were originally introduced to improve punctuality to school and lessons, the school did not anticipate the success of the idea or its growing importance to school life. The 'butterfly' effect has worked really well in that the role of the supervisors has expanded in helping to promote a climate where young people are nurtured in a healthy and positive environment. They are now an integral part of an overall student support team, managed by an assistant head, able to link positively to the community that the school serves and respond quickly to student needs.

Butterfly 9

Praise postcards/birthday cards

Description

When a student has done a piece of work that demonstrates improvement or merit, a teacher fills in the details on a school postcard that the headteacher signs and posts to the parents. These are timed to arrive at the weekend so that the family can receive them together. One school also sends a birthday card to all its Year 7 students as a way of making them feel part of the school community.

Comment on impact

The use of these praise postcards has done a great deal to raise the self-esteem of many students. Parents and carers have enjoyed receiving them and some have commented that when they previously received communications from the school they always expected them to be bad news. Staff have found the cards very easy to complete as the format is already established.

Butterfly 10

A staffroom teaching and learning noticeboard

Description

A special noticeboard is allocated in the staffroom just for articles, comments, cuttings, book reviews, butterflies and so on, related to teaching and learning. In one primary school all the staff take it in turn to provide material for the noticeboard (which is changed every two weeks) and to talk about this during a staff meeting. In a secondary school, subject departments provide the material on a fortnightly rota, but on general teaching and learning issues, not just their subject discipline.

Comment on impact

The noticeboard generates interest and discussion about teaching and learning informally and formally as it is in the staffroom. These noticeboards usually highlight key articles from the *Times Educational Supplement,* education magazines and other sources, as well as ideas that would aid staff development. Sometimes there is also a 'butterfly of the week' displayed.

Butterfly 11

Improved communication between governors and staff

Description

Governing body meetings are held in different parts of the school as a way of communicating and celebrating the specific teaching and learning that goes on in departmental areas. The specialist staff host the meeting and explain the learning environment by conducting a tour of the facilities, making a short presentation and answering questions. This need only take 30 minutes before the meeting starts, and could be followed by a specific agenda item on the learning area concerned. Staff then attend the meeting as observers to learn about the work of the governing body.

Comment on impact

Schools where this has been tried comment on the great gains it provides in helping governors to get to know their school and their staff, and to appreciate different aspects of the curriculum and the processes of teaching and learning. It also affects accommodation and budget decisions. Teachers gain from getting an opportunity to meet all governors, explaining how they work and celebrating their good practice. It gives the governors a chance to be involved in a collective review process that strengthens school development-planning, decision-taking and school self-evaluation. Communication and relationships between governors and staff improve considerably.

Butterfly 12

Learning through action research and case-studies

Description

A school decided to try to promote learning by 'action research'. All staff were invited to form six groups to discuss case-studies of success in the school. Each group identified possible topics, and volunteers wrote the first refinements of practice that might transform something already good into something even better. An editorial group then worked on the text and the results were published as a school booklet.

The school feels that the case-studies are good evidence of self-evaluation in practice, and will commission further studies in order to be able to collect evidence on the way, rather than retrospectively as preparation for an Ofsted inspection.

Comment on impact

The school chose an activity that was likely to increase the store of intellectual activity among the staff, believing that the process would release energy rather than consume it. It is very pleasing to have some rich case-studies that celebrate their successes along the journey of school improvement.

There are, of course, a number of larger, critical interventions that are part of an integrated and focused programme of change, which may take up to a year to implement and perhaps longer to embed thoroughly in the culture of the school. The test is again one of high leverage for such a significant investment in time and energy. These interventions then must be designed to make a distinct difference to previous practice, which will have a significant and measurable impact on student development, learning and achievement, and will need to be monitored and evaluated appropriately. Critical interventions, as major case-studies of educational change, form part of the larger action research programme of a school and are written up and published as a demonstration of the school's commitment to being part of a learning community.

So, even allowing for a wide range of contexts, what do we believe are the critical interventions that are more rather than less likely to increase success?

Promoting pupil progress

Raising standards is the core purpose of any school and there have been enormous improvements in recent years. Most schools are used to reviewing and analysing patterns, trends and anomalies of school performance so that informed priorities and targets can be established. Data on the summative performance of schools is now very sophisticated, with a range of benchmarked information being available from the DfES (now DCSF) through the web-based RAISE online system. However, at present the main school targets focus on achieving improvement measured by end of Key Stage raw averages of attainment. These can be adjusted for the impact of external variables such as pupil mobility, ethnic background or deprivation in the form of contextual value-added data, but this is still a relative measure, only effective when seen in combination with other factors, including raw scores, value added based on prior attainment, school self-evaluation, inspectors' judgements and the content of the school profile.

> Success comes in cans.
> Failure comes in cant's.
>
> Anon.

However, a school can only be considered successful if it promotes progress for *all* students, and good schools are beginning to turn their focus on to this and find measures of individual student progress and of the improvement in rates of progress over time, taking advantage of some of the recommendations of the Gilbert Report (*2020 Vision – Report of the Teaching and Learning Review Group 2006*) and the DfES consultative document on *Making Good Progress* (2006). Schools are examining their assessment policies and procedures and striving to develop better ways of measuring, reporting and stimulating progress so that every student develops at the best pace, and no student gets left behind. Despite the general improvement in summative outcomes and everyone's best efforts to raise standards, students do not proceed, progress or attain equally. Some of the differences in achievement are linked to social and family factors. A student receiving free school meals is currently half as likely to get five good GCSE passes as other students. A student who grows up in care is five times less likely to do so. A student with special educational needs is nine times less likely. There are stubborn disparities among some ethnic groups. There are also problems with underachievement by boys. However, these are just averages of disparity. Within every group of students there is a wide range of variation.

Good schools use the data to focus on better outcomes, with a particular emphasis on raising attainment for every student, regardless of circumstances. They intervene to support a focus on progress as well as absolute attainment by making particular adjustments.

Critical steps:
- Pupils need to know their current *individual* levels of progress, and with their staff and parents plan what they have to do to improve.
- Adjust the approach to classroom assessment and testing to allow a clearer focus on the progress of every individual pupil, often carrying out confirmatory assessments at frequent intervals.
- Personalize teaching and learning to support progression.
- Engage on what can be termed as 'progression tutoring' – individual tuition to lift the performance of those who entered the Key Stage well behind trajectory or seem to be falling behind during the Key Stage.
- Introduce progression targets for individuals and groups of pupils in order to increase levels of performance.
- Make better links between what schools do and what other services do to support the pupil's wider development, particularly in Early Years.

Promoting pupils' progress depends on having an accurate picture of what each pupil can do and intervening promptly if they fall off the expected trajectory, or become disengaged. Good schools develop rapid response systems rather than attempt to catch up long after pupils have fallen behind.

Turning up the power – providing learning opportunities for all children and young people

We know that pupils will benefit considerably from having programmes of tutoring, coaching, mentoring or other personal support at critical moments in their school life. These may involve overcoming a learning difficulty, extending a particular capacity or providing extra learning opportunities to promote greater engagement and motivation for success.

Good schools are constantly reviewing the range of learning opportunities they provide as a means of meeting every pupil's needs and expanding one-to-one learning opportunities. Personalized learning is about helping every child and

The illiterate of the 21st century will not be those who cannot read or write, but those who cannot learn, unlearn and relearn. Our students need to be information literate, lifelong learners.

Alvin Toffler (1990)

young person to do better in order to fulfil their potential and give them the motivation to be independent, lifelong learners. While much can be achieved through more effective teaching and learning strategies, coupled with assessment for learning to identify every student's learning needs, good schools are organizing themselves better to make a reality of the slogan 'Every Child Matters'. They are trying to do their best for every child and young person by adapting schooling to meet the needs of the individual, rather than forcing the individual to fit the system.

Most schools would claim that they give all pupils some individual attention within the constraints of syllabus, curriculum and timetables, but the numbers of disaffected, and often disappeared young people in our schools are a considerable challenge to the school system and to local communities. There is another group of pupils who, though staying with the system, don't respond well to much of the teaching and learning on offer to them. Good schools are constantly auditing their provision and identifying those pupils who need particular support and additional learning opportunities, while also attempting to personalize teaching and learning for all pupils. They are consciously turning up the power by increasing the ratio of adult–child provision and employing a wide range of adults who can offer specialist priorities and opportunities to individual children. Most schools have learning assistants and learning mentors, but there is considerable scope here not just to increase this provision but also to focus the provision more effectively on the specific needs of particular groups and individuals. Similarly many schools have integration assistants and English as a foreign language (EAL) provision, making it possible for inclusive educational practices to be enhanced. Other illustrations of one-to-one provision are peripatetic music teaching, sports coaching, artists in residence, reading recovery tuition and language assistants.

The good school will get most out of the above provision by effectively focusing on and targeting individual pupils, but if the learning power is really to be increased then adult volunteers and peer tutors will also need to be used much more extensively. If the school has strong community partnerships then a range of community leaders, youth workers, sports people and businesses can be used as mentors and role models. Within the school, strong peer-tutoring systems can be developed where 'young teachers' assist 'young learners', particularly in literacy, numeracy and ICT, which can be a significant resource.

To succeed in their tasks of enhancing learning and achievement and turning up the learning power, good schools are seeking new allies within and building new connections to the community of which they are a part. One of the first steps is to build an effective home and community curriculum based mainly on learning partnerships with parents and carers; hence the need for home–school contracts to support learning at home in cooperation with the school, an emphasis on self-directed learning and opportunities provided by the school for parents to enhance their own learning. Parents may sometimes gain formal qualifications in this way, or at least the confidence to learn with their own children. Good schools will partner other important agencies in the community to support learning and services and businesses through which pupils can gain greater economic awareness and an appreciation of the nature of citizenship. The extended schools will first and foremost provide increased learning opportunities with an emphasis on flexible and independent learning, whether through traditional extracurricular activities (such as sport, drama and other clubs) or through study opportunities provided between and after school or at weekends and holidays, such as summer schools. Increased curriculum enrichment and extension beyond the school allows for the greater personalization of learning and extra opportunities to improve motivation and build self-esteem.

Critical steps:
- Audit one-to-one learning opportunities in the school.
- Improve the ratio of adult and child provision to further personalize learning.
- Increase the range of parent, business and community volunteers.
- Develop further the provision of coaching and mentoring for pupils and staff.
- Improve curriculum enrichment and extension.

Unlocking the energy: participation in innovation and research

The personal and professional growth of teachers is closely related to pupil growth. One of the most significant critical interventions a school can make is to invest in learning for all staff and deliberately seek out ways to participate in innovation and research. This can be achieved in a number of ways. It may start from including a commitment to research and further learning in the job-descriptions of all members of staff. From there, one could ask how each member of staff could give a learning example to the school. Is it through the observation of classroom practice, the production of an interactive display, reporting back on a learning experience at a staff meeting or through further, accredited study? Whatever the route, the expectation would be that each member of staff would set a learning example; indeed, would have an annual learning-plan. From this could be developed a more systematic notion of the teacher as researcher. A successful school will always have a planned series of specific reviews that will involve teachers and other staff in critically evaluating current practices.

A secondary school's research and innovation programme for one year:

- An examination of continuity and progression in English through a review of work done in Years 6 and 7.
- Researching attitudes to teaching and learning in Years 8 and 9 through interviews and student questionnaires, in partnership with a local university.
- An investigation into the research skills of particular groups of students using the internet and school library.
- Teaching boys separately from girls in certain GCSE subjects, in order to ascertain the impact on raising achievement.
- Introducing and researching the effectiveness of a mentoring programme for Year 10 students.

All staff need to be able to collect and analyse data and contribute to the research-based culture of school improvement. In this way they will not only be able to reflect on their own practice but influence change within the school generally.

A school geared to innovation and research would have somebody designated as being in charge of research, with possibly a link governor. They would coordinate classroom and whole-school reviews and be responsible for the publication and dissemination of research findings. The school would set a target of publishing its action research at least once a year. Further, it would organize and coordinate an annual learning conference at which other schools and educationalists would be invited to share their findings, and where the key issues of school improvement could be debated and analysed.

The accreditation of learning, whether for parents, lunchtime supervisors, classroom assistants, nursery nurses, school secretaries or teaching staff, would be a major feature of the school's provision. There are increasing examples of schools becoming recognized training bases for NVQ-level qualifications in, for example, childcare and information technology. There are others which are established outreach professional development centres of further and higher education, providing staff with the means to obtain a range of further qualifications.

Crucially, a school of innovation and research would have dynamic partnerships with higher education and the educational research community as a whole. Teachers would undertake further qualifications, with courses provided partly in the school to allow them to improve both their academic attainment and their classroom performance. The school would attract cohorts of teaching practice students who, as well as learning their craft alongside skilled and trained mentors and coaches, would be expected to undertake small-scale research studies concerning the learning needs of individuals or small groups of pupils. They would be expected to present their findings to the school and suggest ways of improving practice. As part of the school–higher education compact, lecturers in teacher-training would be expected to lead staff seminars and workshops and plan joint research activities on a longer timescale with the school. Similarly, 'expert' teachers would be expected to participate in elements of teacher-training. Just as some hospitals are designated as 'teaching hospitals', so the school would wish to be designated as a 'teaching school', focusing on research and innovation and constantly seeking to be more effective.

Critical steps:

- A collective commitment to undertake reviews and publish active research.
- All staff to provide learning examples and annual learning-plans.
- An annual learning conference.
- Accreditation of learning for everybody.
- Teaching and research partnerships with higher education.

The quality and range of small and large interventions is the crucial element in delivering success, alongside how well the school is organized and maintained. Good schools capture and spread their 'butterflies' and carefully plan and evaluate their critical interventions. Their shared culture of professional development, action research and collective review means that they can deliver and sustain success.

Reality check **1**: Running a school is a messy business

Staff . . . pupils . . . and money

One head once remarked to us: 'You both make it sound so tidy. And it's not like that. It's all too often messy and confusing with a lot of dirty business to do.' Of course she was right. Leading a successful school involves many uncomfortable tasks where the head, especially in a small primary school, is mostly alone. Let's take the case of getting rid of the incompetent teacher, or any other member of staff for that matter.

The incompetent member of staff

They come in many guises, though there are fewer of them than when the first edition of this book was published 15 years ago. However, the task is no less unpleasant than it was then. Nothing is more tricky than when, as sometimes happens in a school that's fallen on hard times and is dragging itself painfully uphill under new leadership, the incompetent teacher is the leader of the staffroom cynics. To compound the problem, luck sometimes has it that he is a union representative.

Case-study

'He was never short of an opinion. Indeed he kept an open mouth on everything I did and attributed the basest motives to even the most straightforward of changes', the head remarked ruefully. 'I judged that the rest of the staff individually and in private thought he was a pain in the proverbial, but the feeling that you shouldn't betray a staffroom colleague – even a loud-mouthed and incompetent one – meant that they remained silent in a group situation, especially in staff meetings. So the business of going down the competence route was long, drawn-out and stressful: it took a year and a half what with taking time off at just the right moment to avoid the formal events in the "due process".' She confessed to

$\Rightarrow$

be close to quitting herself at one point, when to her disgust the local authority adviser counselled ducking the issue because of the union connection. In the end, ironically with the support of the regional union official, he left to spend his time on the business he'd set up on the side years earlier. 'It's often the case of course that such people are a pain in other contexts too', the head reflected. 'They told me afterwards they too were pleased to see the back of him.'

Reading between the lines of that story you would guess – correctly – that the school had indeed been down on its luck and had been allowed to decline to the point where professionalism had acquired a new and lower meaning. It was, in short, the sort of place where staff movement had meant that the staffroom was made up of only the very young and inexperienced, who hadn't looked closely enough when accepting a job, or older and increasingly exhausted stalwarts who were serving out their time, unhappily aware that they were unable to obtain another job because of their age and the school's reputation. In such places dealing with incompetence is so much more difficult, partly because other members of staff are thinking 'Is it my turn next?' It is no use reflecting that this feeling is not remotely justified if you are determined to rediscover the pleasure of being among colleagues who are determined to support each other by upholding certain levels of consistency in corridors at break and lunchtimes, as well as in the classroom. You are so trapped in your mindset in that situation that you have forgotten that 'it doesn't have to be like this'.

For the head who is taking on that issue, it's all a question of the finest judgement. What is the best mix of fanning the embers of the few 'energy-creators' in the staffroom and rooting out the 'energy-consuming' incompetence of others, while also getting the barely competent to change gear and start contributing? Judging how many of the 'energy-consumers' to take on at once and in what order will vitally affect the school's progress. Perversely it's trickier, in our observation, where a school is in Ofsted terms 'satisfactory' and just short of a 'notice to improve' or 'special measures'. The external judgement where a school is in an Ofsted category has created a situation where people know change is inevitable and urgent, but when the decline hasn't quite reached crisis-point the impetus to improve can be much more difficult to establish.

This sort of 'messy business' is easier by comparison in the really successful school. The veteran head in an Ofsted-rated 'outstanding' school told us of a comparable incident where even his legendary 'fussiness' in appointments hadn't worked in the case of a business studies teacher.

Because of the very high standards among the staff the person involved knew deep down that he didn't fit. In short, it was a much easier process and much less time-consuming than it would have been in a less successful school.

Pupils

Not all pupils come to school eager to learn and committed to the school. Despite the school's best endeavours some bring such 'baggage' from beyond the school gate that they are well nigh impossible to 'enlist' to the school's values, even to a minimum acceptable extent. This is more the case in secondary than primary schools and very much more the case in those schools that are struggling against the odds and accepting many students at different times during the year ('high mobility' is what is used as shorthand to describe the issue). All secondary schools have the added problem that so often occurs in adolescence, namely as Tom Wylie, the distinguished HMI and recently director of the National Youth Agency has oftenput it: 'They have an absolute determination not to reveal in front of their peers that they are beginners.

They have to be instant experts. More confusing still are those youngsters who have simply given up and seem unreachable. They don't care. They are aggressive and get their kicks from the street rather than the school or the home.

It's in cases like these that the schools can face the dilemma of exclusion. Let's take a case-study.

Case-study

A head and his staff had tried everything. 'We knew Sean was difficult when he arrived', the primary head confessed, 'and that he'd only really survived during KS2. We contained him by having him sit outside the office door for much of his time and "run errands". Of course we gave him one-to-one support too but his confidence and self-esteem among the other pupils was minimal. So when he arrived with us we knew it would be difficult. We organized one-to-one sessions with our SEN experts. Put him in a class, however, with youngsters of his own age and he "blows". Sean is a large lad now too. His mother – there's no Dad – confesses she can't handle him. The absence of a Dad, who in this case is in gaol, has its advantages because so often the macho side of the inadequate Dad means the family is in denial. Anyway, by Year 8 Sean was terrorizing the neighbourhood where he lived, even though he was still just about containable in school. There was talk of an ASBO. We tried everything we knew with him in school: all the things that usually work but nobody could get through to him. You know you say that if a student hasn't got at least one worthwhile relationship with at least one adult in the school he really isn't at school? Well, in Sean's case it was worse because he didn't have a worthwhile relationship with anyone worthwhile outside school either. He appeared to belong to a group of what you can only describe as "feral" boys in his neighbourhood and a junior member of the "Johnson gang" [the head was referring to one of the gangs in that part of the inner city]. The final straw was a vicious attack on a fellow pupil in Year 9. But the exclusion process took ages. And at every step I felt a failure. We hadn't done with Sean what we were sure we could do when he arrived. He'd been on one of our residentials: we'd arranged placement for some days in a nearby community venture, but everything broke down. We tried learning mentors. We'd tried to involve other agencies. But you know how difficult that is: with the best will in the world you find that the reliable person in the police or the social services has moved on and you have to start all over again. The reality was that Sean had grown more and more alienated. We had all failed him.'

The case illustrates the defeat the head felt and the unappealing nature of this aspect of the work. He went on to reflect on the actual process of exclusion and on the difficulties that can so often arise in other disputed cases. There is the legal representation at the hearings that have wrong-footed so many heads, the appeals panels that behave unreasonably and always the need to get the 'ducks lined up' in the correct order.

Once again, as with staff issues, the more securely successful a school is, the less time they will find taken up with 'dirty business'. We have chosen to illustrate this sort of 'dirty business' by incidents involving staff and pupils. However, 'dirty business' is not necessarily confined to people.

The budget

When the first edition of this book was published, local management of schools (LMS) or 'fair funding' as it came to be called, was in its infancy: indeed it hadn't reached those schools where a combination of a reluctant LEA and unenthusiastic or even anxious heads meant that they were postponing its introduction as long as possible. The responsibility for the massive sums involved in schools budgets rested with the LEA and some heads had seen chief education officers depart suddenly when the budget was overspent. Their own 'dirty business' involved avoiding the redeployment of staff from other schools where rolls were falling. Worse still was when a nearby school closed and those staff and pupils who remained were transferred to your school, for, as might be imagined, most of the best staff and pupils had already left the closing school.

Since LMS the question of managing money becoming 'dirty business' seems to us to have occurred most frequently in two circumstances.

The first is the question of the inherited but undeclared deficit where the outgoing head has spent money irresponsibly as he has departed to another school or to retirement. The baptism for the new head is as fiery as it can get, as so often the rest of the school community, including an incompetent bursar, can be in blissful ignorance of the true state of affairs and therefore in denial. More seriously, the very governing body that has so recently appointed the new head needs some convincing that it too has not done its job properly. An even worse variant on this is where there has been dishonesty involving the misuse or misappropriation of funds.

There is probably no general advice to be offered here other than to seek the advice of one of the headteacher organizations that will have been involved in many cases.

The second situation occurs where a head carries the responsibility of managing and trying to arrest the decline of a school losing pupils because it has become unpopular, usually because it is perceived to be unsuccessful. In our experience, such schools have the added problem of having become the school that inherits pupils whom other schools find too hot to handle. Perversely the declining numbers make the acceptance of those 'difficult to handle' youngsters an almost irresistible temptation.

The 'messy business' here involves spending large amounts of time persuading the local authority, and shortly for academies it will be the DfES (or whatever quango it will set up to run its rapidly expanding family of academies), to accept the principle of a sufficient loan as you set out on a recovery plan.

We have chosen to illustrate 'messy business' by reference to examples drawn from matters affecting staff, pupils and finance, but as any head knows it doesn't stop there. There is no shortage of messy business and we might as easily have given examples involving parents and sometimes governors. As we said at the beginning, we were chastened by the head who reproved us for making it sound so straightforward. Our work with struggling schools has convinced us that those outside such schools do not realize the huge and disproportionate amount of time that it takes to sort out 'messiness' as they embark on the long road to success.

3 Teaching and learning

Learning can unlock the treasure that lies within us all. In the 21st century, knowledge and skills will be the key to success . . . Good teachers, using the most effective methods, are the key to higher standards.

DfES (2003b)

The important thing is not so much that every child should be taught, as that every child should be given the wish to learn.

John Lubbock

If pupils don't learn the way we teach, perhaps we should teach the way they learn.

Howard Gardner (1991)

Teaching and learning cultures

The quality of teaching and learning is at the heart of school improvement and real, lasting change can only come from what teachers and support staff do consistently in classrooms and other learning areas in the school. Curiously, although schools have polices for almost everything (partly with an eye on the Ofsted inspection process), some schools still do not have many policies on teaching and learning, and it is sometimes difficult to ascertain from their practices whether those they do have are based on an individual or a collective approach. In successful schools the staff have thought through together what constitutes effective teaching and learning in their particular context, based on a set of core values and beliefs, and they continue to speculate how they might improve their practice, involving pupils, parents and governors in the debate. They are aware that their central purpose and the focus of all their endeavours is raising the achievement of pupils and they engage in collaborative activity to ensure this. Principles are turned into processes and practices, and once agreed strategies have been implemented they are constantly monitored, reviewed and adjusted again in the light of the evidence. Through this process there is an internal dynamic to teaching and learning and the school is geared to continuous improvement. There are high expectations for everybody, as both learners and teachers. The headteacher in particular is a leader of learning. There is, in fact, an apparent teaching and learning culture in the school that is constantly being nourished and developed, with staff taking individual and collective responsibility to improve on their previous best, with reference to the best knowledge and practice available, and committing themselves to regular self-evaluation.

In considering how to improve a school through the development of a dynamic teaching and learning culture it may be best to start from the point of view of the new teacher who, full of hope and expectation (and certainly a little trepidation), joins the staff of a school on a permanent basis. All headteachers and teachers could usefully ask themselves how, simply by joining them, a new teacher would become a better teacher and would strengthen even more the critical mass of effective teaching.

> Educational change depends on what teachers do and think – it's as simple and as complex as that.
>
> Michael Fullan (1991)

We have referred previously to teachers as leaders. The task of schools is to develop their teaching culture so that everybody is an 'energy-creator' for at least part of the time and never less than 'neutral' at other times. The new teacher is therefore energized immediately by simply joining the staff and is caught up in the excitement of teaching and learning. What would be the characteristics of such a teaching and learning culture and how may a school develop this? This chapter discusses the key features of such a culture that, if adopted, would help to improve all schools.

An agreed policy about the practice of teaching and learning

Such a policy would start from the basic question of whether the whole staff, which includes teaching and learning assistants and all those who contribute to the teaching and learning process, have discussed their ideas and beliefs about teaching and learning and how best to raise standards of achievement. The policy would emphasize a shared philosophy and a shared language. It would cover the central issues of teaching and learning styles, teaching skills, the importance of questioning, the place of story in explanation, resources for learning and teaching, and learning as the central concern of continuing professional development and support, as well as self-evaluation and review.

There is a vast amount of research literature on all these topics, but because context is so important it is essential that every member of staff, involving pupils, parents and governors as far as possible, hammers out their values, practices and expectations and makes sure that this overall policy is translated into an appropriate pedagogy at all levels within the school. Subject leaders, whether in successful primary, special or secondary schools, are able to transmit the central messages effectively into their areas of the curriculum and work with groups of teachers on developing appropriate schemes of work and lesson-plans. Teachers working in year groups or Key Stages are able to base their planning on these overt principles, processes and practices, and to monitor and evaluate accordingly. From all this emerges a unity of purpose that is a condition of achieving consistency of educational practice across all staff in the school. A policy for teaching and learning could be constructed under the following headings.

Values, beliefs and principles

- **The development of a shared language** about the craft of teaching and the complexities of learning.
- **Repertoire and range of teaching techniques,** skills and strategies exposition and explanation, practical activities and investigations, the use of questions, discussion and problem-solving; individual, group and whole-class teaching.

Personalized learning

- Tailoring education to individual needs, interests and aptitudes in order to fulfil pupils' potential.

Learning styles

- Awareness of multiple intelligences, the need for differentiation, independent learning and critical thinking.

The use of learning resources

- A range of resources appropriate to pupils' age and needs, provision of information technology, reference materials, the role of the library/resource centre in supporting learning.

The effectiveness of planning

- Continuity and progression of learning, the organization of short-, medium- and long-term planning.

The use of assessment

- Assessment for learning, the marking of work, the use of assessment information to inform curriculum planning, formative and summative assessment.

High expectations and appropriate challenge

- Appropriate tasks and teaching techniques for pupils of different abilities, accelerated learning, setting and banding.

Creating and maintaining stimulating learning environments

- Effective classroom organization, interactive and whole-school displays, a climate of innovation.

Monitoring and evaluating teaching and learning

- The collection of evidence and the critical reflection on polices and practices, action research.

Successful schools, with clearly thought-out and expressed polices and practices on teaching and learning contributing to a dynamic 'learning culture', are able to state these in their recruitment literature and attract like-minded staff with an opportunity to reinforce these beliefs within the induction programme. Perhaps most tellingly of all such schools institute the practice of making sure that all applicants are observed teaching as part of their recruitment strategy. This strategy reinforces the message of the critical importance of quality teaching in the school, but also has the benefit of involving pupils and other staff in the process of classroom observation and teacher selection. Already the new member of staff feels part of an effective teaching culture, simply by joining the staff and being ready to undertake a continuous programme of professional development securely anchored within a teaching and learning policy.

High-quality teaching

One of the features of successful teachers, who are 'energy-creators' that see the glass as 'half-full', a 'silver lining in every cloud' and ask 'What if?', is that they use three or four parts of appreciative enquiry for every one problem they need to solve. Meanwhile unsuccessful teachers, who are 'energy-consumers' that see the glass as half-empty, 'clouds for every silver lining' and say 'What more can you expect from these children?', become enforcers of compliance at the expense of appreciative enquiry as they wrestle with their mounting problems.

The pupils in the classrooms of energy-creators and appreciative enquirers have a much more successful experience than those in the classroom of energy-consumers and enforcers of compliance.

So our first two points about teaching are that:

• the disposition and attitude of teachers are crucial
• important though well-rehearsed classroom management and organizational skills are (including the three-, four- or five-part lesson with plenaries), by themselves they are not enough.

Characteristics and qualities of good teachers include:

• good understanding of self and of interpersonal relationships
• generosity of spirit
• sense of humour
• sharp observational powers
• interest in and concern for others
• infectious enthusiasm for what is taught, allied to excellent subject knowledge
• imagination
• intellectual curiosity
• professional training and understanding of how children learn
• ability to plan programmes of learning appropriate to the particular groups of children and individual pupils and access so that they know how to improve
• understanding of their curriculum in the context of the school as a whole.

So if disposition and attitude are important, what more can we say about them in the outstanding teacher? Outstanding teachers genuinely believe that all children can learn successfully and that they can teach anyone to succeed. They have learning goals for themselves, both for the subject and the way they teach. They are not afraid to involve the learner in the assessment of their lessons. They try out new ideas. Their teaching is therefore a competence to be continuously increased and they develop learning competence in their students. They practise 'assessment for learning', whereby the learner becomes aware of the next stage of learning and knows how to extend the learning already made. These teachers do not so much differentiate the groups they teach, but rather they differentiate themselves. They believe that effort on the student's part in learning is not a sign of limited ability. They make learning fun and exude hope, energy and enthusiasm. They behave as if learning is a cooperative authority – 'We can crack this algebraic problem together, Class 9, can't we?' – and harness learning as a group as well as an individual activity, thereby importing to the classroom (with all the positive messages of collaboration) the gang nature of the playground or the street, where its consequences are often negative and disastrous. Above all, they believe in the 'transformability' of their students as opposed to their ability.

Teachers work on the cusp of the axis between 'self-esteem' and 'expectation'. If expectation is too high and the students' self-esteem too low, the students will fail to learn and the teacher fail to teach. The other way round, that is students' self-esteem ahead of teacher's expectations, is almost as serious. We say 'almost', because in these circumstances older students with higher-order learning competence will learn despite the teacher. The issue is to pitch expectation, both for the group and for the individuals, just a bit ahead of where the students have reached.

> It is the supreme art of the teacher to awaken joy in creative expression and knowledge.
>
> Albert Einstein (1950)

So all teachers work at self-esteem. They greet students positively in the morning and speak to them by name, not just in the classroom but in the corridor and at lunchtimes. They create a shared past and tell good stories about their students, who know they are expected to contribute to the 'legacy' of the school. They share in the interests of the young, whether that is celebrities, soaps, sport or food. They remember birthdays, recognize the achievements of students elsewhere, whether in the school or beyond the school. They mark privately and confess to a private interest. When a student baffles them and when they can't, as it were, make contact, they seek out an article or artefact at the weekend that they know resonates with the student's interest. Then they quietly give it to the student with the words: 'I saw this and thought of you.' In short, they are masters of the unexpected. In their students' eyes they appear safely and interestingly unpredictable.

In the field of expectation they use story, are expert in questioning techniques and involve their students in leadership.

Outstanding teachers ensure that their pupils are at least as busy as they are! Pupils, after applying for various jobs as classroom managers, know it's their job to monitor attendance, to mind the computer, to organize resources, to collect in books at the end of lessons or whatever. Teachers in such classrooms deploy a marking practice that makes pupils feel special. They provide extensive private written feedback to each pupil at least twice a year. They are such masters of 'assessment for learning' that pupils become able to assess their own and other people's work. In doing so, their pupils become more and more active and competent, autonomous learners.

We think that the whole teaching process can be likened to a golden cracker. In the golden cracker there are essentially three parts. The first involves getting to know the students – their likes and dislikes, their hopes and ambitions, their strengths and weaknesses and their preferred learning styles. The second and central part of the cracker involves a student practising skills, doing exercises, being occupied gainfully in consolidation of learning, while the teacher becomes proficient at classroom control and involved in the refined arts of planning and organization. The third and most vital end of the cracker is the teacher's extraordinary skill as an alchemist of the mind, endlessly surprising students into doing and understanding things they never thought they could do. At this end lies the golden cusp of the teacher's skill: her ability to open the mind, often a part of teaching that is least analysed and discussed. It is particularly connected to the skills of questioning and speculating for students with different sorts of intelligences and at different stages of self-esteem.

> To be a passionate teacher is to be someone in love with a field of knowledge, deeply stirred by issues and ideas that challenge our world, drawn to the dilemmas and potential of the young people who come into class each day, captivated by all of these. A passionate teacher is a teacher who breaks out of the isolation of the classroom, who refuses to submit to apathy or cynicism.
>
> Robert Fried (1995)

> Teachers affect eternity, they can never tell where their influence stops.
>
> Henry Brook Adams (1918)

Questions, questions

Much has been written about sequencing, distribution and the rules of pause. Some schools, however, only ask pupils to put their hands up in certain prescribed and thought through circumstances, preferring the teacher to direct questions of an appropriate nature to different pupils according to where they've reached in their learning. Other schools, wishing to ring the changes, have a 'question monitor', with the teacher posing the question, again carefully considered as to difficulty, and the 'question monitor' taking one of the 30 sticks, each with a pupil's name, from a beaker.

Teachers are expert in four orders of question, each using the seven questioning words: 'when', 'where', 'what', 'why', 'who', 'which' and 'how'. First-order questions are questions of fact; second-order questions are questions of influence; third-order questions are 'surprising' questions; and fourth-order questions are ones of 'conditional hypothesis', preceded by the devilish 'if'! We sometimes think 'surprising' questions are the same as 'Fermi' questions. Fermi was an Italian nuclear physicist who loved complex questions. An example of a 'Fermi' question would be: 'How many piano-tuners are there in New York?' They are designed to call for lateral thinking, estimation and justification of your hypotheses that lead to your conclusion. Equipping pupils with knowledge of the seven questioning words and the four orders of question paves the way for good group-work, because pupils are skilled in using questions.

In addition to 'questions', teachers may look at each other's 'story-telling' techniques, for as we have remarked, stories are at the very heart of successful teaching, since the mind-opening habits of the philosopher Plato.

Also, what of the 'alter ego' of teaching? Just as the nursery teacher sends teddy bears home to have adventures with pupils, who come back and create pictures and stories of what's happened, so the same teacher uses the teddy bear as another character to stimulate pupils' talk. The primary teacher continues this practice for a time and is alert to the use of puppets. It also continues into secondary school, not in the form of puppets, but sometimes with lifelike figures in the history room (Henry VIII, say) or in science (for example, Darwin), and to these figures the teacher from time to time defers. They have imaginary conversations on the phone and, in the digital age, have orchestrated 'e-tutors' to whom the students can turn. One school has an enthusiastic teacher who has his very own 'Avatar', a constructed and moving figure on the screen with a programmed voice. We are, of course, in the foothills of our journey to exploit the learning technologies.

In one school, teachers debated, agreed to produce and then created a booklet for all students called *Language to Think and Learn*. Based on theories of multiple intelligence and the need for variety of learning approaches, the booklet set out the vocabulary for each subject (and for examinations) that they wanted the students to understand – high-order conceptual language, if you like. All the staff then set about teaching the meaning of the vocabulary, week by week, to the students in Year 7. A similar approach has been adopted in Years 8 and 9 – the whole issue of course reinforced by display of the vocabulary in every room.

Personalizing learning

In successful schools the staff have thought through what constitutes effective learning in their particular context in order to raise the achievement of all students and put into place appropriate processes and practices. They will be aware of the dangers of young people's learning being dominated by judgements of ability that can profoundly affect their self-esteem and sense of identity. Students learn very quickly about their standing in comparison with their peers, and which category they belong to in terms of 'more able', 'average' and 'less able'. This kind of learning is often reinforced daily through many different kinds of experiences, and it takes a conscious effort to practise 'learning without limits', so that young people's school experiences are not all organized and structured on the basis of judgements of ability.

Personalized learning is about helping every child and young person to do better, which means tailoring education to individual needs, interests and aptitudes so as to fulfil their potential, and giving them the motivation to be independent, lifelong learners. For schools it means a professional ethos that accepts and assumes that every child comes into the classroom with a different knowledge base and set of skills, as well as varying aptitudes and aspirations.

Components of personalized learning:

- *Assessment for learning*
  Understanding where each pupil is in their learning, giving quality feedback and planning the next steps with shared objectives.
- *Effective teaching and learning*
  Developing the competence and confidence of every learner by actively engaging and stretching them through the systematic and explicit development of learning skills and strategies across the curriculum.
- *Curriculum entitlement and choice*
  Delivering breadth of study, personal relevance and flexible learning pathways through the system.
- *Organizing the school for personalized learning*
  Using more support staff and specialist expertise in order to remove barriers to learning and create the conditions that are needed to ensure that all pupils can make the best progress possible.
- *Beyond the classroom*
  Extending learning outside school to meet the needs of pupils and their families and build strong partnerships to drive forward progress in the classroom and to support pupil well-being.

These five key components are integrated and mutually supportive. The use of ICT permeates all components as a way of enhancing creativity and extending learning opportunities.

The Specialist Schools Academies Trust, in a series of pamphlets on *Personalized Learning* (2005–6) edited by David Hargreaves, suggests that schools approach the task of personalized learning through nine interconnected gateways.

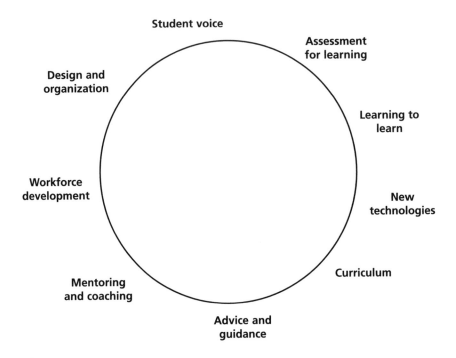

Figure 4 The gateways to personalized education

The overall impact of the gateways on students can be understood as a sequence of core themes or strands that capture what characterizes the pupils for whom learning is being successfully personalized. These core themes are

- engagement of the pupil in learning and schooling
- the responsibility assumed by the pupil for learning and behaviour
- independence in learning
- confidence in learning
- maturity in relationships and pupils taking ownership of their learning.

Schools will recognize this agenda as trying to do their best for every child and young person by adapting schooling to meet the needs of the individual, rather than forcing the individual to fit the system.

Most schools would claim that they give students individual attention, but those that are working hard on personalized education have realized that there is a lot more that they can do, particularly in allowing students opportunities to work at their own pace. Choice is also an important part of personalized learning, particularly in secondary schools, with the building of individual learning pathways. However, the constraints of syllabus, space curriculum and assessment can make it very difficult to offer a truly personalized form of learning, although there have been some innovative approaches through the benefits of workforce remodelling and more effective use of ICT. In the last analysis 'the curriculum' must appeal to the individual or the group. In the end, the successful learner is engaged in the curriculum that the teacher has tailored to the world. For example, teachers have rightly criticized the 'one size fits all' National Curriculum and National Strategies because they are overprescriptive and de-skill teachers by discouraging them from bringing their own views to the curriculum, even at the margin.

It also needs to be recognized that the school day and the school year provide only a small percentage of available learning time. That's why the suspended timetable involving a 'day' or a 'week' of learning is so important to successful learning.

> Instead of a National Curriculum for education, what is really needed is an individual curriculum for every child.
>
> Charles Handy (1997)

To succeed in their hope of enhancing learning and achievement, schools must find new allies and build new sorts of connections to the community of which they are a part. One of the first key steps is to build mainly on learning partnerships with parents and carers, remembering that they are co-educators of children in tandem with teachers (something that we cover in Chapter 6).

The most important attribute that schools can give students is the ability to learn on their own and to take responsibility for their own learning. While this can be encouraged through the formal curriculum in terms of flexible learning and independent learning, the provision of curriculum enrichment and extension opportunities creates a real opportunity to prepare for lifelong learning, whether through traditional extracurricular activities – such as sport, drama, chess and other clubs and societies – or through study opportunities provided before and after school by breakfast clubs or at weekends and holidays – such as courses and residential learning experiences, Easter revision courses, summer schools or study extension with organizations such as the Children's University or Gifted and Talented Centres. Curriculum enrichment and extension allows for a greater flexibility of teaching and learning, particularly around techniques such as accelerated learning and concepts such as multiple intelligences. There are also extra opportunities for developing information and communication technology skills. Above all, an improving school will provide these opportunities to improve motivation, build self-esteem, develop effective learning and raise achievement.

Learning styles

The concept of learning styles has become a cornerstone of good practice, although not without its critics. The most commonly used system in schools is the VAK model of classification, which divides children into visual, auditory or kinaesthetic learners: those who like to look, those who like to listen and those who learn best though physical activity, sometimes called 'active learners'. Most learning styles analysis relies on self-assessment questionnaires completed by children. This has obvious defects. Many school activities are not purely visual, auditory or kinaesthetic , but a mixture of all three. Even if we accept that children learn in different ways, most teachers agree that a preferred learning style is simply an acquired habit and that children need to experience other styles. Most schools that embrace the concept of learning styles try to encourage teachers to make lessons accessible to all students by including visual, auditory and kinaesthetic elements. They believe that it is equally important for teachers to analyse their own style of learning and teaching. Most teachers, they argue, allow their own style to become their habitual teaching style – to the detriment of those students who learn in different ways.

The danger with other rigid classifications of children's learning preferences is that children will be labelled and forced into a narrow view of their own abilities. However, some mechanisms for assessing learning styles take a more holistic view and look at a wide range of issues under the heading of 'Learning Styles'. For example, the Learning Style Analysis profiles promoted by the publisher Network Continuum are based on a wide series of questions grouped under categories that are brain-based, sensory, physical, environmental, social and attitudinal. These profiles (which are accessible online) are based on the research work of Professors Dunn and Dunn of New York in the 1980s, and now developed into electronic format by Professor Barbara Prashing of Auckland, New Zealand. The outcomes or profiles avoid labelling children by describing preferences and flexibilities in the spectrum of issues involved. Nevertheless, it seems that learning-style models are still an oversimplification of the complex way in which children process information. However, the debate over learning styles has at least encouraged teachers to examine their own practice and explore a wider repertoire of teaching strategies. Perhaps instead of talking about learning styles, we should talk about learning skills and provision of an environment most suitable for learning, whether that is individual, group or class working, the availability of learning technologies or aural stimulation.

Assessment for learning

Personalized learning is closely linked to the assessment of students, in the sense that you cannot tailor learning unless you know about student progress. However, the emphasis here is on assessment for learning, rather than assessment of learning, so that students can improve on their achievements and make progress. There are different ways of achieving this, but the rationale is always the same. You need clear evidence about how to drive up individual attainment; clear feedback for and from students on what they need to improve and how best they can do so in order that learning intentions are shared and criteria for success understood. It is also necessary to involve pupils in the ownership of their learning, through self-assessment and peer-assessment.

Assessment for learning is not new, but as richer data have become available, it has become a more important and sharper tool, aided by developments in technology. Good schools recognize that this is not an occasional activity at the end of a unit of work but an ongoing joint activity between teacher and pupil. Teachers gain information that helps them adjust their practice, while pupils increase their understanding of their progress and of the standard expected. Most teachers are familiar with many of the elements of assessment for learning and respond flexibly to their pupils' needs. However, where there is a whole-school context that establishes the priority of assessment for learning, supported by effective systems for tracking pupil progress, the impact of assessment on learning is likely to be considerable.

Learning technologies

Making the most effective use of learning resources is a great challenge for schools and integral to any discussion about learning and teaching. There are key policy issues that need to be worked through, including individual access to information technology; the personalization of learning; the design of classrooms and learning areas, including the library/resource centre. The long-term development of student responsibility and independent learning requires an institutional approach, as does the development of the role of the teacher in managing resource-based learning. Teachers need to be seen increasingly as managers of learning and less as presenters of information. In this context the use and management of learning technologies is fundamental to effective learning and achievement.

Good schools will have a strategic view on the place of ICT across the curriculum, and improved access for all learners. When students come to school many, though not of course the disadvantaged few, leave the wired-up world of their home where access to television, video and computers is commonplace, to enter a building where ICT learning resources are still not extensively employed in everyday learning, although new technologies are making considerable headway. Thankfully, in a society and economy where ICT is transforming the way we live and earn our living, all schools are radically re-examining how students should be learning, not least because of all that we know about how students learn at different rates and in different ways. Schools of this new millennium will have a vision of how to use shared intelligence rather than relying simply on teacher intelligence, although they will never forget that good teaching inspires the best learning. Full use of the new learning technologies helps teachers and support staff to create a learning environment where students can build actions and create knowledge, something that can be carried on within the home and the community. Learning through ICT, including email addresses for staff and students, will enhance and enrich the curriculum and its assessment, offering new and exciting opportunities for individual learners to access a wider range of quality learning programmes and materials. A good school takes full advantage of the fact that everybody in the learning community can create, receive, collect and share text, images and sounds on a vast range of topics, in ways more stimulating, richer and more time-efficient than ever before. They have begun to exploit the possibilities of 'co-production', which the new wave of 'up-loading' technologies allows (see the second reality check for further explanations).

Pupils taking ownership of their learning

We have stressed the importance of pupils:

- coming to a shared understanding of learning goals and how to achieve them
- developing the skills and attitudes to become better learners
- establishing through the pupil voice the habit of talking about learning and teaching and how to improve it are equally important.

Schools have a central role in helping pupils to develop the skills and attitudes for learning, and some have developed their own 'Learning how to learn' programmes or used programmes such as the RSA *Opening Minds*, progressing through mind-maps to research skills allied to use of the internet.

Several researchers and writers have referred to 'learnacy' or 'learning power' variously defined as:

- Resourcefulness in the sense of being able to learn in different ways.
- Resilience in the readiness and persistence in learning, reflectiveness in being able to become more strategic about learning.
- Reciprocity in being able to learn alone and with others.
- Responsiveness in being able to adapt to different styles of learning. Others have stressed the particular importance of emotional intelligence in learning how to learn.

In encouraging learning we always have to pay regard to the 'cognitive' and 'affective' domains, explained beautifully by Sir Alec Clegg (1980) as 'loaves' and 'hyacinths' (see p. 90). In this context Clegg explained: 'The loaves are mainly concerned with facts and their manipulation, and they draw on the intellect. The hyacinths are concerned with a child's loves, hates, fears, enthusiasm and antipathies, with his courage, his compassion and his confidence.'

Teachers and other adults in school have an important role in setting clear expectations and modelling positive attitudes to learning, giving young people exposure therefore to a wide range of contexts and role models for learning, along with experience of genuine responsibility. They will recognize that learning takes place everywhere using a broad range of resources – cultural, social, financial and physical – and make sure that pupils can take ownership of these opportunities.

With regard to the pupil voice, good schools are engaging pupils actively in shaping learning and teaching developing 'learning conversations' between teachers and pupils, as well as between pupils. Some examples of this are

- asking pupils to provide feedback on particular lessons after training them as observers of lessons

- involving them in participating in the SEF process with regard to surveys on the quality of teaching and learning
- involving pupils in the selection process for new members of staff
- using pupils as learning resources for one another and helping their peers to learn and develop, within the classroom and beyond.

To help pupils take ownership of their learning, schools are changing some of their organizational structures so that the workforce is more geared to personalized learning. Primary schools have supplemented the role of the class teacher with learning assistants and learning mentors, and some secondary schools have developed the idea of the 'learning guide', a person who gets to know individual students over a period of time, works with them to establish and review their learning needs and monitor their progress, and is able to act as an advocate for them. The role of the learning guide is different to that of coaches and mentors in that the focus is quite specifically on how the student is progressing in their learning, rather than tackling particular issues. Such a system guarantees that every student will have at least one person in school who knows them, knows what they are learning in school and beyond and understands their learning needs in the round, and can then jointly agree targets for their learning and reviewing progress across a range of indicators.

Improving learning

Learner characteristics are not fixed: previous experiences and previous competence and beliefs influence present learning. Learning can occur through multiple channels and through different learning styles. Learners vary in their beliefs about success and in their motivation for learning. The school, as the key site, of institutional learning, models effective learning by encouraging the personalization of learning within a climate of high expectations, joint learning and shared responsibility for learning. They know that effective learning takes place where pupils can acquire and use a range of learning skills, integrate prior and new knowledge, think critically and solve problems individually and in groups. Schools that become professional learning communities are better able to connect with learning out of school, so that their children and young people can become effective, enthusiastic and independent learners committed to lifelong learning and better able to cope with the demands of adult life.

The Gilbert Report (2006) identifies the best practice in teaching and learning and makes some key recommendations:

- All schools should reflect a commitment to personalized learning in their learning and teaching policies and plans, indicating the particular strategies to be used.
- Schools should identify their own strategies for embedding assessment for learning.
- Schools should consider how best to ensure that their curriculum supports personalized learning.
- Schools should consider how best to integrate 'Learning how to learn' into the curriculum – focusing on the skills and attitudes pupils need to become better learners.
- Schools should consider how best resources within the school, such as the new technologies and the physical environment, might contribute to fulfilling their commitment to personalized learning.
- Schools should consider all those pupils and groups not making progress in any Key Stage and as a result put in place progress plans to overcome barriers to learning.

The celebration of teaching and learning

As we said at the beginning of the chapter, our new teacher joining the school would become a better teacher just by being on the staff if there was an agreed policy about the practice of teaching and learning, and a culture sustaining quality teaching and learning. In such a culture pupils and adults alike would be engaged as active learners, encouraging everyone else's learning.

The *Times Educational Supplement* for some time had a weekly column on the subject of 'My Best Teacher', and it is interesting to reflect upon the qualities that are most often commented on by past pupils. The articles reaffirm the joy of teaching and learning and remind us all that we can instantly recall from our own experience the teachers who were enthusiastic, committed and caring, who treated everyone fairly and who were interested in us as individuals. We remember our best teachers as those who made learning exciting, were good communicators, were very willing to help and obviously enjoyed their jobs. We also recall their spontaneity, humour and mannerisms. Above all, we remember them as passionate teachers who liked children, loved learning and had the capacity to touch our hearts.

In his book *The Passionate Teacher* (1995), Robert Fried argues that for teachers:

Passion is not just a personality trait that some people have and some others lack, but rather something discoverable, teachable and reproducible, even when the regulations of school life gang up against it. Passion and practicality are not opposing notions; good planning and design are as important as caring and spontaneity in bringing out the best in students.

In the really successful school everybody benefits from coaching and mentoring within a shared culture and understanding of the processes of improvement. Having a shared vision is vital for learning organizations because it provides the focus and energy for learning. It is noticed by the new teacher that the school is often visited by other headteachers, teachers and advisers who are eager to see at first-hand the effectiveness of teaching and learning in the school, and to participate further in the debate to make this even better.

A walk around any successful school provides further opportunities to question, speculate and analyse. The classroom and all learning areas and spaces make their contribution to the joy and excitement of the learning process. The rhythms of the school day and the school year provide for enhanced teaching and learning opportunities and for learning and teaching celebrations. The school community has clearly thought out ideas on learning assemblies, opportunities for independent study in the library or particular resource areas, the development of study skills and the provision of one-to-one learning opportunities to overcome a learning difficulty or extend a learning talent. Information and communication technology enhances opportunities for pupils, teachers and parents to learn from each other, as well as through particular programmes and the internet. Curriculum extension and enrichment opportunities provide for year-round learning through residential experiences or the opportunity to join other pupils in learning organizations providing after-school and vacation learning experiences. In short, the school endeavours to provide success for everyone – staff as well as pupils – by providing people with multiple entry-points to success and opportunities to celebrate success.

Features of a learning school

In summary the features of a learning school are as follows:

- *Personalized learning*
  Helping every child and young person to do better through tailoring education to individual needs, interests and aptitudes so as to fulfil their potential and give them the motivation to be independent, lifelong learners.
- *learning-plans*
  All members of staff have an annual learning-plan, as well as a portfolio, to help them improve their skills.

- *Learning styles*
  A recognition that children and adults learn in different ways, which is reflected through pedagogy.
- *Learning habits*
  Integrating 'Learning how to learn' into the curriculum, focusing on the skills and attitudes pupils need to become better learners.
- *Learning conversations*
  A planned and systematic approach to professional dialogue as well as dialogue between staff and pupils.
- *Learning walks*
  A focused approach to discovering best practice within the school, as well as through hosting and visiting other schools.
- *Learning guides* (mainly for secondary schools)
  Based on the principle that all students should have at least one person who knows them and what they are learning, learning guides agree targets for learning, monitor progress and can act as an advocate within the school.
- *Assessment for learning*
  Understanding where each pupil is in their learning, giving quality feedback and planning the next steps with shared objectives.
- *Learning forum*
  Meetings for staff particularly interested in innovative approaches to teaching and learning where pedagogy is explored, shared, tried out and then discussed.

We started this chapter by affirming that the quality of teaching and learning is at the heart of school improvement, and we have described some processes and practices that enable any school to secure continuous improvement in this area. In particular, we have stressed the importance of the establishment and development of an effective teaching and learning culture that is constantly being energized through staff and pupils taking responsibility to improve on their previous best. In this sense good schools are always in the making, taking their mission very seriously and developing their own internal dynamic related to:

- unquenchable intellectual curiosity with reference to fields of knowledge and pedagogy
- a relentless drive towards attaining higher standards of achievement for all pupils
- a huge commitment to building confidence, competence and self-esteem among all learners
- passionate teachers and staff, whose goal is always the highest quality of learning experiences for pupils.

A school teaches in three ways; by what it teaches, by how it teaches, and by the kind of place it is.

Peter Senge (1990)

4 Continuous professional development

Like any skill or craft, learning to teach is a developmental process characterised by devastating disasters and spectacular successes. Teaching is a job that can never be done perfectly – one can always improve.

Sara Bubb (2005)

Teachers teach, but unless they learn constantly, they will be unable to perform their central role in a rapidly changing society.

Michael Barber (1996)

Continuous learning for everyone is central to the notion of the intelligent school.

B. MacGilchrist, K. Myers and J. Reed (2004)

Recruiting, appointing and developing staff

All school improvement involves change and development. However, the experience of change can be individually threatening or disconcerting so we need organized settings and systems in schools that support staff in the process of change and make it more rather than less likely that school improvement will occur and good and outstanding schools develop. We know that the continuing professional growth of teachers and support staff is closely related to improved school outcomes, so creating opportunities for staff to learn together will make performance better and more consistent throughout the school. Good schools enhance capacity from within by building and extending professional learning communities. They are learning organizations in which everybody is engaged in the understanding and development of effective practice.

These schools recognize the importance of establishing a positive climate in the sense of establishing trust and

> A learning organisation is an organisation that is continually expanding its capacity to create its future.
>
> **Peter Senge (1990)**

openness between staff as well as pupils and the community. Success is celebrated, decision-making is an open process and communication is clear.

To build and extend a professional learning community that can transform pupil achievement requires the development of a high proportion of 'energy-creators' on the staff who

- are enthusiastic and always positive
- practise leadership at all levels
- stimulate and spark others through working in teams
- use critical thinking, creativity and imagination
- are able and willing to scrutinize their own practice and to make their practice accessible to others
- believe they can improve on their previous best.

Above all they are aware of being a role model to colleagues. These 'energy-creators' can demonstrate their leadership qualities by working alongside other staff in helping them to raise their game or to connect better with opportunities to develop and improve their practice. One of the secrets of good and outstanding schools is that they help ordinary people behave in a way that is extraordinary.

A key indicator of any school is how staff – teachers and support staff alike – behave one towards another, as well as with the pupils. Are they cheerful, optimistic and full of ideas and good humour, or are they grumpy and cynical?

Successful schools seem to be agreed that you are looking for three things in staff:

- a competence in the job
- the potential and disposition to improve (whether from average to good or good to outstanding)
- that they should be of the 'right disposition'.

You know you are in trouble when you visit a school and encounter 'Well what more can you expect from kids from backgrounds like this?', or when an explanation for an acknowledged deficiency is concluded with the phrase 'You know how it is.' The energy-creator will be tempted to reply 'Well, no I don't know how it is. Explain why it is!'

The very best schools know that they can sometimes turn an 'energy-consumer' into an 'energy-creator', but all are agreed that it's best to avoid that challenge if it is at all possible to do so. And that brings us to the question of appointments . . .

Being fussy about appointments – it starts with the advertisement

If our aim is to have as many energy-creators as we can, the advertisement can have the effect of attracting the right and repelling the wrong candidates. Lively 'further particulars' laced with humour and illustrations of school life will attract the 'can dos' a school is seeking to attract. They will certainly put off those who are cynical. So will conversations with staff who can and do recommend working at the school and often tip-off the senior team if asked about possible promising candidates. Of course Ofsted reports are available and read by applicants . . . 'certainly the ones we want', as one head put it. Clearly the school with a glowing Ofsted report starts with an advantage, but if the further particulars show that a school with an indifferent Ofsted report is regarding it as a 'wake-up' call and clearly shows its determination to change gear for the better, the best candidates will not be put off.

Case-study

'I am upfront about our determination to move from "satisfactory" to "good" and "good" to "outstanding"', a head who was shifting her school in the right direction, thanks to the good staff she had been able to appoint, told us. 'But', she went on, 'it's the interview process that makes or breaks it.' She, like many other heads, would never dream of making an appointment of a teacher at any level in the school unless she, other staff and of course pupils had seen them teach and provided feedback. 'It would be the equivalent of a football manager signing a new player without having seen him play', she went on, reminding one of us bleakly of the apparent habits of the football team we support. She also takes similar care with every appointment of support staff by providing them with situations where they can demonstrate their skills. 'Everyone is vital to our school. For instance the receptionist makes our job easier or more difficult through the telephone and how you are greeted on arrival. So we certainly don't want to get that appointment wrong. I try to provide them with questions that require the candidates to root their answers in what they have done in their jobs or in life as opposed to what they say they will promise to do.'

Time and again successful headteachers, and of course their trusted colleagues who take on the role, will say when reflecting on specific posts: 'It took us a long time to find Ms Scott for the science job', illustrating their fussiness by reference to the number of times they went through the application process before finding the right person.

All agree too that to 'appoint in haste, or even when not entirely sure, is to repent at leisure'.

Another device favoured by schools is to become involved in initial teacher education, either through being a member of a group of schools running a school consortim for initial teacher training (SCITT) or in the graduate training scheme or, more often, by partnership with a university in a school-based PGCE scheme. 'It's like a long and thorough interview process. We never make offers to the wrong newly qualified applicants', confessed a Stoke-on-Trent head, who over ten years had recruited a third of her staff through the local PGCE scheme.

Getting job-descriptions right

Any member of staff needs a job-description when appointed. How that is framed is also of crucial importance in encouraging energy rather than exhaustion. We have referred to the need for that in Chapter 2. It is so important and so often overlooked, we think it bears repetition.

The wisest schools ensure that the contracts for their teachers emphasize no more than two or three principal accountabilities (matters for which the teacher is the lead person in the school) and three or four secondary accountabilities (matters on which the teacher is a supporting person in the formulation of policy). Those are the important matters: they will give the teacher the energy to contribute to the whole life of the school and in doing so they will also offer the teacher fulfilment and satisfaction.

A sample job-description

Apart from taking part in the whole professional life of the school, which is committed to successful teaching and learning and requires of all members of staff tutorial responsibility and the support of others in the usual administrative matters of the school, you have the following principal accountabilities:

- Taking the lead in conjunction with departmental colleagues in establishing mathematical priorities and practices of the school.
- Ensuring, in conjunction with departmental colleagues and the school's administration, that the department is adequately staffed and resourced.
- As a result of the above, establishing with colleagues and the curriculum leader of the school agreed criteria to show how progressively more students in the school may develop their mathematical talents.

You have also the following secondary accountabilities:

- Contributing appropriately through the school's curriculum review process to the overall curriculum development of the school.
- Taking the lead from time to time, with agreed criteria for planning, organizing and reviewing one aspect of cross-curricular work.
- Taking part in some aspect of extracurricular activity.
- Monitoring in support of Ms Julian the effectiveness of the PSHE programme in the upper school.

Different schools use different language according to the climate they are seeking to encourage for those closely related activities and the emphasis they think appropriate for individual staff discussions.

As we said in Chapter 2, in the best schools job-descriptions are provisional and subject to review and change after a specified period. In this way, leadership can be reviewed and rotated for the benefit of the individual and the schools as a whole.

The staff induction programme

Of course, the essential details for the staff induction programme – the underlying policy and the details of the practices – will be included in the staff handbook. But it is worth picking it out: it becomes a vital support to maintaining consistency where there is high staff turnover. Staff induction must encompass all staff, teaching and support alike. It should contain a common element for all with faculty-based (including administration team function) elements. The timetable will usually be on an annual cycle. It will offer opportunities for those who arrive either at the beginning of the school year or during it, to have a brief, repeated general introduction. This should be followed by a sequence of modules, carefully focused on what the school knows are the vital elements in 'singing from the same song-sheet'. There is, in addition, a guide for part-time and supply staff, so they too know what it is they are expected to do to support the school.

Staff development . . . leading to successful teaching and learning

When we talk of school staff or the staffroom we automatically think of teachers. It is arguable that *some* of the most vital members of the staff at a school are not teachers at all: many teachers have wryly commented, 'If you really want to find out what is happening in the school it is best to ask the caretaker or the school secretary.' The comment, which at face value is about communication systems, conceals a more fundamental point. After all, the business of the school – whether it concerns problem pupils, awkward visitors, the administrative support system, the arrangement for trips, meals, ordering equipment and supplies, dealing with the LA, the diocesan authorities or the DCSF, even the governors' meetings – all tends to go through the office. Indeed, if the headteacher knew as much about the detail of the school as the secretary/administrator/bursar, they would not be doing their job properly.

While on the subject of support staff, what of the skills and duties of the now long-established midday supervisors? There is little doubt that their skill, coupled with the impact of the external environment at lunchtimes, has had a profound effect on the incidence of bullying in particular, and the behaviour of the school in general. So the wise school gives a high priority to the development of midday supervisors' skills and attitudes. The whole primary school looks to extend their hours to work with individual pupils one-to-one either side of the lunch-hour: in secondary schools some have become 'learning mentors'.

So if the teachers are the people who mainly contribute to a school's main business – namely unlocking the talent of future generation – it is wise not to forget that support staff have the potential to contribute significantly to that task. Nor is the contribution exclusively behind the scenes. How pupils are treated in the school's office, how support staff talk to pupils in the corridor or on the way to school, how they deal with confidences, all affect children's life chances. What is more, as it is almost always the case that more of such staff than teachers live in the locality, their messages to the local community about what is really happening in the school are crucial. If what follows, therefore, has teachers mainly in mind, it is because their morale is more vulnerable. At every stage, however, it is necessary to stop and ask whether the same issues affect all members of staff.

Teachers get exhausted where the rest of us merely tire

Teachers know that the inflection of their voice, the movement of an eyebrow and their attitude every minute of every day when they are with the pupils affects those pupils' ability to learn. And they are in contact with the pupils a lot. So it is that teachers get exhausted where the rest of us simply tire. Learning is the whole business of the school: it deserves to be in the forefront of the minds and conversations of all in school, who nowadays need to guard against displacing learning by managerial or organizational topics such as 'resource management', 'external relations' and so on.

Unlike teachers, the rest of us (including headteachers) enjoy 'down-time' when we are properly involved in activities that do not require us to give of ourselves perpetually: we can work in private, albeit briefly.

All staff require four conditions to be satisfied if they are going to carry out their duties effectively. They need

- responsibility
- permitting circumstances
- new experiences
- respect and recognition.

Let us look at each individually.

Responsibility

Most people confuse responsibility with work. We quite like the former but are liable to get stressed by too much of the latter. Most of us, with the increased pace of communication, particularly in written form and with the expansion of knowledge, are not short of work. Indeed, from time to time all of us feel helpless about the things we should have read but haven't. It is particularly difficult for subject-teacher specialists, for they have seen their own field of specialism transform itself within a very short space of time, often just a year or two. Publications have proliferated to an extent that it is virtually impossible for a serious scholar to be aware of the content and impact of all that has been written in his or her subject. This point was brought home vividly on a recent Radio 4 programme about the life of J.B.S. Haldane, when experts agreed that for that very reason (i.e. the expansion of specialist knowledge) we should not see again the likes of Haldane. It would simply be impossible for one mind, however exceptional, to be at the frontiers of knowledge across so wide a field and to translate that knowledge in a popular form. Therefore, there is a far greater stress on teachers than in previous times, when advances in knowledge had not accelerated to the same extent.

Because those in schools tend to be idealists, their inability to cope causes enormous guilt. Thus it is as well for schools to be clear about the difference between work, of which there is too much and which causes a feeling of guilt, panic, helplessness and inadequacy, and responsibility, which is often badly distributed. Responsibility for something is, after all, having the final say about it: it is taking the lead and providing a vision of how things could be.

Of course the whole issue of responsibility, as we have emphasized, is best tackled at the time people are appointed. The work undertaken in preparing a background 'position statement' for job applicants and the principal and secondary accountability list for the particular post is vital. Moreover, it needs to be shared among all staff. We particularly admired the school that devoted a part of the school noticeboard entirely to that purpose, so that as jobs came up, the fruits of the preparatory work were regularly displayed. The deputy in charge would draw the attention of the whole staff, as the occasion demanded, to the details for the new vacancy. In that school the process of appointment meant that those involved in the newcomer's principal and secondary accountabilities would take part in some aspect of the interviewing and appointment process, even when there was only one applicant.

The school had a system for knowing who was responsible for what, and there was an open system of appointments. There were, of course, different ideas about how it could be improved, but all recognized that what they had was a better system than they had encountered elsewhere. Significantly, one of the improvements under consideration was the extension of it to support staff. Let us be clear. They had a similar system but the jobs were not displayed on the noticeboard. Moreover cross membership involving teaching and support staff in appointment processes is at a very tentative stage, but they argue that it is bound to improve the staff's shared sense of common purpose.

Permitting circumstances

Once teachers (and others) have their responsibilities made clear, they desperately need 'permitting circumstances'. At its simplest this has an obvious meaning. If there are no books, materials or equipment, then the opportunity to teach well is, to say the least, restricted. So the link to the environment (see Chapter 5) is obvious and of primary importance: it is analogous to the basic human need of food and warmth.

Four very important matters sometimes get neglected.

1 *Teams*

First there is the need to ensure that teachers can work in teams: that means not merely the obvious clustering of subject-interest rooms so that resources are shared but also how whole year groups will be registered.

- Within departments is there the facility for team-teaching if it is needed?
- How can the department or faculty head have the physical help to build teamwork?
- Are there noticeboards that show the intellectual curiosity of the faculty?
- If there is emphasis on the home group or the year group, how are those activities physically fostered?
- Can dining or social areas be used to the advantage of the teaching team effort, either of the department, the year/home or the school?

2 *The staffroom*

Secondly there is the question of the staffroom. Here we shall make enemies. You can gain a pretty strong clue to a school's success by its staffroom. If there is the issue of 'peer-group pressure' among pupils, so there is among staff.

There used to be the bridge corner in our early years of teaching. It was great fun but it was the enemy of real thought and debate. It was succeeded by the snooker table and the dartboard. Some people will say we exaggerate. We do not. Quite simply the staffroom conventions, even the walls, are a barometer of a school's success. Conversations can be dominated either by backbiting or by debate about children's progress. There can be social chatter with no cutting edge, or debates about interests that might inform the school's progress. Walls can be the repository for the cynical cartoon or more positively the latest 'thought-provoking piece' about some educational matters. Bridge, darts and snooker – and let us be clear, we are devoted to all three – shouldn't dominate. That is not to say that there shouldn't be some provision for that. Why not provide perhaps a separate social area available to staff, parents and pupils alike as part of community practice? It shouldn't be in a staffroom, however.

3 *Support staff for teaching and learning*

The third point of neglect in teachers' physical permitting circumstances has been their access to a unit staffed by support colleagues who are devoted to the production of materials to support their teaching and children's learning. It is bound up with the question of resource-based learning, or flexible learning as it is now sometimes called. Teachers will find that the use of such approaches will be considerably enhanced if there is a unit properly organized and devoted to their service. So many good plans in that direction have foundered on the organization and provision of non-teaching backup to the best-intentioned of schemes. The same problem exists where large schools fail to staff adequately the library or resource centre. One school we know had a facility for all teachers to be videoed 'privately' so the strengths and weaknesses of their pedagogical style could be reflected upon at leisure and in private if they so wished.

4 *Taking risks*

It is important that teachers are encouraged to take risks. There is, however, something far more important to teachers' permitting circumstances than the physical. Put simply, do teachers work in surroundings in which it is permissible – even encouraged – that they should try out new ideas? After all, in unlocking any child's mind they need to keep afresh their sense of intellectual curiosity: they need to be pushing back the frontiers of their knowledge of how some children learn and how information skills and attitudes can be learned and developed more successfully. The best teachers take risks, and when they do, they need to know they will be supported. One headteacher we know put it simply by saying that she really hoped that the staff would take risks, but that when it was really risky and might get her into a fix either with parents or governors, they would tell her. She would not stop them, but she would be prepared to back them up. Amazingly she would remind them occasionally that she hadn't been taken to the limit of saying 'no' for some time.

New experiences

The third aspect of staff development is the need of all staff for 'new experiences'. People need new experiences to keep intellectually stimulated. To some extent, of course, that happens in the classroom or in departmental meetings or in whole-school activities. It can be a new job: certainly to make a career in simply one set of school surroundings is less broadening than to have experience of three, four or five different settings. Teachers and others argue long and hard about 'fly-by-nights' or people 'who think only of their career' to denigrate those who hop from one position to another without ever staying long enough to prove anything. Certainly a stay of less than three, four or five years in one set of circumstances is unlikely to mean that you give as much as you receive. Get much beyond seven, eight or nine years, however, and there is a real risk of becoming stale.

Case-study

Mrs Hughes is the head of a primary school. When she arrived she inherited staff, one of whom had been at the school in the same classroom for at least eight years. It was a place where they sat in the staffroom in the same chairs. All were in their mid 30s and 40s. After she had talked to all of them individually she didn't have to prompt three of the staff, who separately asked if they could do something more than teach the same age children in the same room in the same way for the next 20 years! It was natural and easy, by teaching their classes herself, to get the three to start discussions on the various differences between the 6, 8 and 10 year olds respectively, which happened to be their responsibility. Soon they suggested a change of teaching for a year. Before long two other members of staff were asking to have the same opportunity. Even the remaining three could be persuaded to change classrooms.

At secondary level such changes are easier to engineer either at the departmental or school level simply because the school's timetable will require some change of teaching experience from year to year. In one secondary school some of the responsibilities are swapped every three years so that new eyes can be brought to the development of the same problem. Often this is restricted to the senior management team of three or four or five. It is perfectly possible, however, to design principal or secondary accountabilities that can be shared at all levels of staff management. It is necessary to be quite firm about the need for colleagues to try something new. Otherwise there is a real danger that work is something that is done almost on autopilot and that the only sources of stimulation and new experiences come from experience outside home.

Of course, you know you are a winner when you find members of staff who, off their own bat, ask if they can try out something new in the school, either as an extracurricular club or as a different set of teaching experiences. Moreover the teacher we met before the summer holidays, sitting on a wall in a Stoke-on-Trent high school, was a headteacher's dream. She was off to the deserts of America for her summer holidays. She said, 'It is part pleasure but part of the need I feel to have vivid experiences which will excite my teaching in the forthcoming year.' In exactly the same way you will be able to spot the long-suffering spouse of a primary teacher who is always collecting things on holidays. They see their life experiences as an aid to teaching.

Above all, however, it is essential to enter a plea for a proper set of experiences under the broad heading of 'What Teachers Need', just like any other staff, to give the stimulation of a fresh slant on old ideas and the chance to learn new skills.

Nothing is more important than the role of 'professional development coordinator', often given to an assistant or deputy head. Yet it is sometimes the most neglected and incoherent aspect of school life. All too often somebody in the leadership team is allocated the responsibility as an 'add-on' to many others. They are the person to whom a member of staff will go to ask for a grant to attend a course. The function is cursorily reviewed, if at all, and is not subject to Ofsted close scrutiny.

We believe that if the government would invest imaginatively and long term in professional development, and perhaps ask the National College for School Leadership or the Training and Development Agency (TDA) to come up with a range of 'best practice' school-based models, the current and periodic crises in leadership succession planning and in supply of shortage subject teachers would be a thing of the past.

There is also the issue of the best use of the five INSET days. This precious time can be wasted in a collective collusion supposedly to allow departments to catch up on things they are behind with; in other words, to do 'their own separate thing'. Is it any wonder that we complain about the silo-effect of the department? There is another way. They can be used, as one school has, to allow staff to visit in twos and threes different schools that are in session while they have taken their occasional day, to learn more about an agreed school or faculty priority. Faculty, phase and staff meetings are used as follow-up and everybody observes the 'six-month' rule that results in a standing professional development day agenda item, which seeks honest review of what has changed as a result of previous visits, courses and visiting speakers.

In London, as part of the London Challenge, we have overseen the introduction of the Chartered London Teacher (CLT) scheme. We proposed the scheme on the basis that newly qualified teachers in the inner city needed more knowledge and competence in the five areas of teaching, subject knowledge, school improvement, cultural awareness (for example EAL, faiths and so on) and overcoming barriers to children's learning. That is to say, we argued perhaps contentiously, that an inner-city teacher needed more than a counterpart in a more affluent and mainly homogeneous area. So we asked that a candidate for the CLT should accumulate a portfolio of evidence for each of the five areas. They would be rewarded with £1,000 provided their school testified to their growing competence and confidence.

Of course the real reason behind the scheme is to increase the likelihood that teachers keep alive their intellectual curiosity and not allow it to shrivel in the crises and pressures of the everyday life of an urban school. Over 38,000 enrolled and many are going on to register for their Masters degrees, mostly in some practical aspect of school life. There is so much more that could be done at a national level to set a positive climate for professional development. But the individual school can achieve more in successful professional development than is possible at local authority or national levels.

We have already shown that schools can and do use their five INSET days to great effect. The following case-study – not unusual – shows how a school has 'commuted' two of its five days to ensure a regular fortnightly school-based staff development programme.

Case-study

The school is a large secondary school in south London. Every other Thursday – it has a fortnightly timetable – the pupils arrive not at 8.45am but at 9.10am so that a brief period of staff development can happen between 8.25am and 9.10am. One day we witnessed the event. The maths department was illustrating how they had used a video to capture all the departments teaching of one of the nine key concepts they thought essential to master to get a higher grade at GCSE. All gave a whole-class explanation that was slightly different and had agreed which two of the explanations should be archived. 'We had a debate about "explanation" linked to effective story and imagery of course.' They had then put the best two for each concept on DVD and stored it on the school intranet (which was shortly to be converted to an e-learning platform. 'In this way', they explained, 'we have at least two alternative good explanations for them to try when one of our students still can't understand it after our repeated and patient efforts to help! It's also useful for students who have been away and have missed key lessons.' The same department has a clear agreement of what are 'key' lessons and a surgery after school for students to drop in for extra help to understand the issue.

The person responsible in the senior team for professional development declared that two other departments were taking on the idea. It would probably be included eventually as one of their agreed features in the 'Whole-school teaching and learning policies and practices', which was a kind of bible to ensure consistency of approach across the school.

Another school in east London has an extensive programme published for all staff at the beginning of the school year of events that have taken place after school on Wednesdays. 'I make sure that on appointment all staff are encouraged to take part. We get in visiting speakers, but the best sessions are run by our own staff, all of whom through a departmental focus are a part of a research climate', is how the head described the scheme, as she went on to add that the sessions always ended with a good buffet.

All these schools spend a fair proportion of their budget (2 per cent in one case) on staff development of one kind or another, and such schemes include all staff, not just teachers. They evaluate its effectiveness and how the staff rate it on a regular basis. They know that it's a systematic way of encouraging and sustaining 'energy-creators'.

Case-study

A secondary school decided to accept a greater contact ratio (85 per cent) in order that one member of staff could be released as a 'float' to support a regular release of staff from a particular departmental area, in order that the department concerned could pursue its own plan to develop the curriculum. This was achieved by visits over a year to other schools, the culling and preparation of information and teaching materials and the adoption of some new approaches to learning and teaching. The same scheme rotated to different departments and has been going for seven years.

Case-study

A primary school of four teachers had a headteacher who had half a week teaching commitment. She used one morning of the other half of her week to take 60 pupils with volunteer parents on a planned dramatic production, while the two released teachers visited schools together and planned a joint curriculum change. During the second half of the day (also part of her non-teaching time) the same headteacher spent teaching one of the groups while the two teachers concerned, returning from their visit, taught the other class together and compared notes.

There are other subtleties, and all these case-studies provide a glimpse of the many ingenious ways schools use to keep alive the flame of their staff's intellectual curiosity.

Respect and recognition

The fourth need of staff is for respect and recognition. Simply because teaching is a fairly isolated activity its success needs to be recognized. There is sometimes little respect and recognition for teachers, which the following lovely poem from the *TES* so graphically illustrates:

'Who'd be a teacher?' is what we've all said.
When at something past midnight we've crawled into bed,
And thought of the morrow with certain misgiving;
This can't be the best way to earn me a living.
'Who'd be a teacher?' I'm sure you've exclaimed,
When once more in the papers the teachers are blamed
For hooligans, drugs and graffiti, and crimes;
It must be our fault – we've been told enough times.
'Who'd be a teacher?' It just isn't rational,
And now we must all teach the curriculum national;
Targets are set, and each child we'll test.
And teacher will know what to do with the rest.
Who'd be a teacher, when some half-witted pundit
Gets a half-witted theory, and a half-wit to fund it.
Then duly announces 'Your methods are wrong;
Children learn best if you teach them a song'.
'Who'd be a teacher?' We don't need more pay,
Just look at the length of our holiday;
And the hours aren't bad, nine until four;
So why aren't they queuing ten deep at the door?
'Who'd be a teacher?' Well, I've no regret
That I'm leaving, I'm willing to make a small bet

There's a smidgeon of envy in those remaining,
Who know in the future there'll be more complaining.
Who'd be a teacher; we all know the score;
Trails and frustrations we've all had, and much more.
But we've all felt the glow when a child has succeeded,
And the pride that we've helped to give what that child needed.
'Who'd be a teacher?' I'll make a confession,
I'm proud that I've been in this great profession.
And on this occasion I'll raise my glass –
'To teachers – God bless them – they're top of the class!'

(Jennie Radley, former headteacher of Simms Cross Country Infants School,
Widnes. The poem is reproduced with kind permission of the *TES*.)

So how can all staff be respected and recognized? Clearly most of it has to come from within the school. First there is the planned visit by the headteacher to classrooms and departments: there is the seeking-out of matters to praise, both by a handwritten note of thanks and the spoken word. At staff meetings the wise leader will always seek to find ways to thank colleagues by name for particular contributions. There is also the governors' meeting. There is the need, for example, to ensure that the chair of governors seeks to praise the staff as well as the headteacher when there are public occasions.

It would be easy to elaborate on all the techniques of good management of interpersonal relationships. It is, after all, the one quality required above all others as we implied in Chapter 1. It is certainly the key to staff development.

Set aside a time each day for thanking people. People's personal needs require the utmost thought, backed by a good system, to make sure the thought is translated into action. You simply cannot leave to chance that you will regularly remember to have a word with a person and to thank them. One of the best leaders we know used to set aside a quarter of an hour each day specifically for the purpose of writing notes to people about things he had observed that were good or that people had told him were. Once the climate of positive reinforcement is established, it is much easier to pick up on the occasional point of criticism that is, of course, always best done in private. Every now and then we will need that jolt too.

Respect and recognition, however, in successful schools are not merely a 'top-down' process. It is particularly important among peer groups. Staff can make their own lives more enjoyable simply by resolving to do things for each other. There is a social cement in staffrooms that is as intangible as it is real: it comes from shared social occasions and the climate where it is more rather than less likely that staff will simply want to spend much more time together. After all, the outcome is a much pleasanter working atmosphere.

In all this talk of staff development it will be noted that so far we have not mentioned staff appraisal. That is simply because we have not yet met a successful school that over a sustained period has a staff appraisal scheme that would reckon it has been instrumental in affecting positively their success. Nor, significantly, is it highlighted as important in the research in USA, where studies on effective schooling have a long history and there is much experience of appraisal.

The 'collective' and the 'individual' needs: helped or hindered by performance management?

We have already referred to the vital need to balance the collective needs of the school as a whole with those of individual members of staff. At the time of the first edition of this book, 'staff appraisal' was all the rage. Now it's 'performance management'. Both walk the tightrope between enough 'appreciative enquiry' and too much 'problem-solving'. The tension between the two is outlined in business psychology by Cooperrider and Srivasta (1987) in a way that is readily recognizable to school staff, especially teachers. The theory is that you need at least three parts of 'appreciative enquiry' for every one of 'problem-solving'. Each runs through four stages as follows:

Appreciative enquiry:

1 Identify what is good in 'what is?'
2 Ask how it would be possible to have more or extend it.
3 Dialogue and search for other practice.
4 Support action to follow up. (Ask 'Why not?')

Problem-solving:

1 Identify a need or problem.
2 Analyse causes.
3 Brainstorm possible solutions.
4 Decide on a plan of action.

The danger with both staff appraisal and performance management is that people tend to dive in with too much of the latter and not enough of the former, causing both defensiveness and a loss of energy. (Clearly the first creates energy and the latter uses it.)

'Whatever it's called', a veteran of three headships in 24 years told us, 'the thing I've found useful is to start with the really good things that we have noticed together during the year, because I always find apparently informal occasions during the year to reinforce what's been agreed at the more formal sessions.' Interestingly the same head saw it as her duty to train every member of the leadership team in the art and science of good conversation/interview technique.

So in effect there are three aspects of this process that good schools emphasize:

1 targets
2 objectives
3 success criteria.

Too many of these externally foisted on you can drive a person mad! But some that are mutually agreed are vital if one of the agreed values of the school community is 'learning' and in the process 'improving on previous best'. In doing so, probably an interpretation of the 'appreciative enquiry' versus 'problem-solving' theory would be to look for 'hyacinths'.

Looking for 'hyacinths'

Every member of staff has a private and professional set of interests they burn about. It might be some aspect of what they teach: it might be an interest such as photography, travel or music. None of these may, of course, relate to what they actually teach. But they are what energizes them and lights up their lives. Whatever it is – and it may be found in what they did many years before in another school – it needs to be given full rein either in their teaching, some other aspect of school life or both. Out of its revival, and with a sufficient diet, what we would call the 'hyacinth' will both fuel that contagious enthusiasm which is the hallmark of the outstanding teacher. But it will also provide the fuel to deal with the many 'loaves' we have in our lives.

We use the images of 'loaves' and 'hyacinths' from a story which Alec Clegg, the Chief Education Officer of the West Riding, used to tell as justification for getting greater balance in the curriculum. As a teenager, he would visit his aunt in Grantham, where the young Margaret Roberts (later Thatcher) would take her private extra language lessons. On the wall was a sampler, which read as follows:

> If thou of fortune be bereft,
> And of thine earthly store have left
> Two loaves, sell one and with the dole
> Buy hyacinths to feed the soul.
>
> Molish Eddin Saadi,
> *Garden of Roses*

Successful heads avoid stress and burnout in themselves and their staff by being keenly aware of their hyacinths and ensuring they have enough of them.

The second and last sentences seem to resonate with the very successful headteachers whom we have met and whose observations and examples have led to this publication.

When you are next ground down by an interminable and complicated appeal or suffer some other unfair blow which might tempt you to ask 'Is it all worth it?' remember the piece by Shaw, perhaps have it framed on the wall, and resolve to find your hyacinth at once.

Our weaknesses or points for development

With the advent of the 'learning technologies', often implied by the initials ICT, most of us can cheerfully sign up to the proposition that we are always going to have areas of our activity where a greater facility on our part would help us in our work. Nowhere is this more the case than in school, where the accelerating developments are transforming learning, teaching, managing and communication. There's a case for arguing, as one school has, that it needs to be an item for discussion not just in performance management but also in the review of departments or phases, as well as the whole school SEF (School Evaluation Form). We are not, of course, arguing that ICT will be the only item – far from it – but we are identifying that it illustrates well the sequence of moving from 'unconscious incompetence' to 'unconscious competence' via 'conscious incompetence' and 'conscious competence'. Linger too long in 'conscious incompetence' and people become fearful and lose heart. Go through the same four-part process on every occasion and people become exhausted. The secret is to keep people learning all the time so that their skills don't become moribund.

> This is the true joy in life, being used for a purpose recognised by yourself as a mighty one . . . being part of a great enterprise rather than a feverish selfish little clod of ailments complaining that the world won't devote itself to making you happy. I want to be thoroughly used up when I die, for the more I work the more I live. Life is no brief candle to me. It's a sort of splendid torch which I've got hold of for the moment. I want to make it burn as brightly as possible before handing it on to future generations.
>
> George Bernard Shaw,
> *Man and Superman*

Preconditions for effective CPD

In considering all the above, we think that there are some essential preconditions for the establishment of the best continuous professional development (CPD) and learning communities:

1 *That there is an agreed school policy about the practice of teaching, which is subject to continuous review.*

   The policy emphasizes a shared philosophy and a shared language about learning and teaching. It covers the central issues of learning styles, teaching skills, assessment practices, inclusion, as well as resources for learning. The key messages of the overall policy are transmitted effectively into every area of the curriculum. Staff working in year groups, Key Stages or subject departments can base their planning on these overt principles, processes and practices, and monitor and evaluate accordingly. There is a consistency of educational practice across all staff in the school founded upon values and beliefs about the complexities of learning and the craft of teaching connected to high expectations and appropriate challenge.

2   *The school, and in particular those in leadership positions, continually emphasize the importance of the study of learning and teaching as the core business of the school.* There are some obvious manifestations of this such as a staffroom noticeboard dedicated to the practice of learning and teaching where everybody takes it in turns, either individually or as a department, to provide appropriate materials such as newspaper articles, book reviews and generic teaching resources. Further there is a staffroom resource area where staff can gain easy access through ICT key texts and information to help them develop their practice. The learning and teaching policy is displayed, along with the priorities outlined in the school development plan. There is an annual publication of case-studies of the best practice in learning and teaching based on action research with an expectation that staff will wish to contribute. There are also collections of 'butterflies' on various themes such as starting lessons, plenaries, the best use of ICT and so on. Also available in hard copy and online is a collection of reports that staff have written after returning from courses, conferences or visits to other schools. These reports are written to an agreed format so as to easily inform everybody's practice. Perhaps most crucially no staff meeting ever takes place without the first item being devoted to some aspect of learning and teaching.

3   *Collaboration is supported and fostered. What makes a good school now is the crucial ingredient of collegiality among the staff, initiating, supporting and sustaining improved learning and teaching.* Good schools have the organizational capacity to work productively both as groups and subgroups to ensure high-quality learning for all pupils. Collaboration is not left to chance or even goodwill but structured through the development of teams and teamwork, study groups, reference groups and cooperative planning, teaching and assessment. The successful school will have a commitment to sharing and designing planning for learning and the preparation and dissemination of learning materials. The more that staff work together in appropriate teams, the more that a shared understanding emerges about the complexity of learning and teaching with the aim of impacting significantly on pupil achievement.

> Good schools grow good teachers.
>
> Judith Little (1981)

4   *As part of staff development in any successful school there will be well organized coaching and mentoring involving pairs or small groups of staff working together.* We are familiar with the role of mentor as applied to new or trainee staff, but less familiar with the concept as applied to other staff. We need to be clear here about the

distinction between mentoring and coaching. Coaching gets beyond general advice and personal support to the specific enhancement of skills in learning and teaching. Good schools have explicitly identified their coaches, commonly acknowledged as outstanding practitioners or advanced skills teachers, and skilfully matched them to other staff with the explicit purpose of improving delivery and raising standards.

5 *Action research and professional reflection is the norm rather than the exception. In an effective learning and teaching culture there will be an expectation that staff, either individually or collectively, carry out action research and disseminate their findings so that practice is continuously evaluated and improved.*

Teachers are natural researchers in the sense that all teaching is based upon enquiry, and the response of the pupils and the pupil voice generally provides ready evidence as to the effectiveness of various learning and teaching methods. The school could commission additional research from groups of staff and pupils to find out what works best in its particular context and thereby provide the evidence to make adjustments to policies and practices. Clearly, even good schools are not successful for all pupils, and it would be important to identify from formative and summative assessments those pupils and groups that are not experiencing success in their learning. For example, why are boys falling behind girls in particular learning activities and subjects? Does the school know exactly why this is? What is it doing to find out more? How can the school rectify this? Some of this action research could be done as part of a school/HE link and it could contribute to a staff accreditation programme such as the Chartered London Teacher, where all teachers have to provide a 'professional reflection', or it could take place on a smaller level as part of everyday practice.

6 *Performance management and continued professional development are integrated.*
Performance management is crucial, particularly at assessment stages, especially as teachers have more responsibility for their own CPD. Within a culture of action-planning and target-setting CPD needs are recognized and shared. Whole-school CPD is then based on this to meet both whole-school requirements and the personal needs of individuals. The new teaching standards provide areas to look towards, especially the way they are set out as a progression model. Using these standards alongside the future-based planning model through performance management objectives, staff can plan for, and define, development needs. Where CPD personal development plans lead to an 'excellent' teacher, advanced-skill teacher and senior leadership posts in particular, staff are encouraged and supported to identify appropriate development needs and links to succession planning. Examples might include special expertise in curriculum development, experience of new school structures, expertise in the 'Inclusion' agenda and success in improving particular provision.

School improvement is most surely and thoroughly achieved when, according to Little (1981):

- Teachers engage in frequent, continuous and increasingly precise *talk* about teaching practice . . . building up a shared language adequate to the complexity of teaching.
- Teachers frequently *observe* each other teaching and provide each other with useful feedback.
- Teachers plan, organize, monitor and evaluate their work together.
- Teachers *teach* each other the practice of teaching.

Good and improving schools are learning organizations in which everybody is engaged in the understanding and development of effective practice as a continuous process. All staff have to be advanced learners in order to develop new skills and insights. David Hargreaves has written about 'intellectual capital', which embraces the education and training of individuals with allied concepts to cover a broader spectrum – their knowledge, skills, capabilities, competencies, talents, expertise, practice and routines. Schools are evidently rich in the intellectual capital provided by the teachers and staff, but also of the students, their families and communities. It is the capacity of a school to mobilize its intellectual capital that is crucial, for this is what fosters new ideas and creates new knowledge in making the school more effective. It is the personal and professional growth of teachers and support staff that will have the most impact on pupil development and achievement. If we take the example of the new teacher joining the school, she will be somewhere on the continuum from beginning to expert teacher, and it is essential that the received culture of learning and teaching is flexible enough to take the teacher forward. With all the preconditions referred to above, our new teacher should feel that she is joining a learning school where staff are able and willing to scrutinize their practice and make their experience available to others, and where everybody embraces a culture of continuous improvement. Continuous professional development and school improvement are intimately related in the sense that they increase a school's capacity and performance, provided that this is grounded in a collaborative culture of values, beliefs, policies and practices.

There are four aspects of teachers and staff as learners that must be seen in combination:

- the improvement of skills
- the capacity to analyse and reflect upon practice
- the ability to investigate, explore and collect evidence
- the confidence to receive and give ideas and assistance.

It is the right of every teacher as part of their continuous professional development to observe other teachers and be observed themselves as a collaborative learning activity. In good schools this process is often organized around 'learning threes', where staff take it in turn to teach, observe and chair the reflection afterwards. If the lesson doesn't go to plan teachers should see this as an event to be learned from, being open to constructive criticism and ideas for improvement. All this is part of the development of a collaborative teaching culture where everybody is a staff-developer, gaining confidence from peer observation in the form of confirming their strengths and improving weaker aspects of their practice and having access to appropriate coaching and mentoring.

Good schools model, promote and support professional development by providing a wide range of opportunities for learning. Many of these are internal to the school, such as peer observation previously mentioned, but there are many others including skills workshops, subject-development sessions, professional discussions, learning walks, participation in action research projects, joining working groups and team-teaching. There will be a proliferation of opportunities where there are positive and open learning environments and this will encourage the acceptance of a shared responsibility and accountability for successfully planning and operating learning experiences. This will have an impact in terms of raising standards. It should also encourage a sense of personal responsibility for professional development, which is one of the aims of the new performance management system. Although we have stressed the importance of school climate and systems in supporting professional development as part of developing the infrastructure of a professional learning community, individual members of staff do need to take full advantage of these permitting circumstances so that the school keeps up the momentum of improvement. One way of doing this is for staff to have an annual, individual learning-plan that identifies the skills to be practised and developed, the particular learning experiences to be undergone, leadership development to be experienced and work-shadowing opportunities all aligned to the overall performance management system. Certainly all staff should be capable of developing an extensive portfolio based on the new teaching standards, which will help them build a career proposition as a contribution to leadership development and succession planning generally. Good schools do grow their own teachers but they also grow their own leaders. In these schools most staff are eager to progress their careers. They will seek internal development opportunities but also to accredit their learning with other bodies such as subject associations, professional associations, the General Teaching Council (GTC), the National College of School Leadership and higher education institutions.

Annual learning-plan:

- *Work-shadowing*
  For example other teachers within the school such as the deputy head, the literacy coordinator or the special needs coordinator.
- *Developing skills*
  For example using particular aspects of information technology in teaching, learning to use questioning more effectively, learning to differentiate more precisely.
- *Learning experiences*
  For example leading a task group and reporting findings, undertaking some action research, leading a parents' group on some aspect of the curriculum.
- *Learning targets*
  For example attending specific courses and conferences, to read the research literature around a particular aspect of teaching and learning, to write an article for publication, to achieve a further qualification.

Although we have concentrated in this section on building a professional development culture within the school, we also have to acknowledge the importance of working together between and beyond schools. No school can provide all the CPD opportunities from within its own resources, and indeed it would quickly become ineffective if it remained isolated from good practice elsewhere. To that end many primary schools in particular have joined 'networked learning communities' sharing their learning and expertise, such as joint staff development days and events and focus-learning walks in different schools. Secondary schools which are now overwhelmingly 'specialist' have worked with specialist organizations such as the Youth Sports Trust. Other schools have developed learning partnerships through local authority groupings, sometimes based on 'families' of similar schools, and others have set up their own websites and have sought to make connections through ICT with similar schools elsewhere. Going on external courses and conferences can move forward knowledge, thinking and practice considerably and it also offers the opportunity to network with other teachers and broaden horizons. However, it is crucial to feed back the learning into the school through a written report or presentation so that everybody can gain.

The litmus test for successful CPD is that any member of staff becomes a better professional just by being on the staff alone, sustained by a culture that promotes the best quality learning and teaching. In such a professional learning community, learning is a stimulating experience with a staff full of energy-creators showing infectious enthusiasm and commitment encouraging everyone else's learning. The staff celebrate their success through their conversations, through their shared language in various groups and meetings, and through their intellectual curiosity as they debate the best ways to improve their practice. In the school there is a generosity of spirit as expert staff mentor and coach others, and there are opportunities for all staff to lead the debate at certain times. There is sense of success when teachers feel confident to talk with a supportive group about what they were learning to do better, as well as what they did well. There is also a collective pride around belonging to the staff of such a school, reinforced by the achievements of pupils, the publication of action research and the recognition of individual and collective expertise beyond the school.

If we take these particular features of schools with successful teaching and learning policies leading to higher standards, the central ingredient is that of collegial, continuous professional development. Good schools have more than competent individual staff. They have organizational and intellectual capital to work productively as a group for high-quality learning of all pupils. Their collegiality is the most important blend of a 'learning-enrichment' school rather than simply a 'learning-improvement school'. The school as a professional learning community has been built and developed through induction, joint planning, joint learning, coaching and mentoring, as well as finding, researching and sharing the best practice, and evaluating the evidence. The bedrock of this culture is the values and beliefs that bond a community of like-minded people together in the common commitment of continuously improving practice and raising standards of achievement for pupils.

> Imagine that you could become a better teacher just by virtue of being on the staff of a particular school – just from that fact alone.
>
> **Judith Little (1981)**

Behaviour, buildings and the created environment affecting school climate

5

What the best and wisest parent wants for his own child, that must the community want for all its children. Any other ideal for our schools is narrow and unlovely; acted upon, it destroys our democracy.

John Dewey (1916)

Rebuilding our schools as places of beauty that also work

The present exercise of rebuilding schools – the so-called 'Building Schools for the Future' – has meant that for the first time for a generation there's a real debate about what school buildings should be like. In the immediate postwar era there was a brief period when new school buildings were built for what were described as 'the children of returning heroes'. That soon gave way to cobbling together 'system-built' schools that were quickly erected in the 1960s and 1970s as a postwar baby boom demanded some sort of school buildings, however imperfect. And imperfect they were, both in the floor area in which to teach and learn and in the flimsy construction materials and design. So, as we all came to appreciate, the flat roof soon sprang leaks and as the cladding rotted, window frames fell out. As they say now, these schools (as we all painfully found out) were not 'fit-for-purpose'. They made the job of schools much more difficult. 'Surround them with things which are noble' declared one famous Victorian headteacher, and indeed we have to go back to that era to find a generation who were mindful of the need to create school buildings that should appear to most of the children as grander than the home surroundings in which they lived; for that's how Victorian school buildings must have appeared to the boys and girls who attended them.

'Building Schools for the Future' offers the chance to do the same. We shall return to the possible pitfalls that the project faces in the final chapter. In the meantime let's start with the impact on ethos and climate of school buildings, of the behaviour of people within the buildings and more widely of the visual and aural environment.

The importance of the physical appearance of a school was brought home when recently one of us was a judge of a re-run of the *Guardian*'s famous 'The school I'd like' competition, which inspired Edward Blishen's equally famous book of the same name around 30 years ago.

The judges had sifted the final shortlist of 40 or so of the thousands of school pupil entries the competition had inspired. It was a salutary experience: one of the most vivid was from three Year 8 students, all boys. Their school was a 1960s system-built, steel-framed cluster of boxed and connected buildings in a sea of tarmacadam, with a moat of a drive through a small windswept muddy field. The video left little to your imagination, as we visited the usual squalid lavatories, the desolate flaking corridors and doors and the litter-strewn playgrounds. It was sustained for ten minutes by a humorous commentary from the 13-year-olds. We paused to meet only one adult, the motherly librarian, working in an environment that contrasted with the rest of the barren school: a welcoming adult in a beautiful oasis of calm. The film ended with a 'zoom-out', incorporating all the glass and rotting wooden clad and panelled building with the words, 'in our ideal school, all of this would be the library'.

It didn't win but one of the entries that did gave a similar message, as follows:

My ideal school could never exist. There is no reality in idealism. I dream of happiness and learning united. I dream of no interruptions. If I went to my ideal school, I wouldn't wake up every morning and dread the next day, the next week, the next year and the rest of my life. In my perfect school, we would only have the teachers who knew and understood what they were talking about. They would all be passionate about the subjects and help us to unleash our passions. In my perfect school there would still be rules, but they would guide us, not confine us. Teachers and pupils would mix harmoniously. There would be no grading, praise only for working hard not for your mental capability. I wouldn't have to try to compete with my friends and they wouldn't all want to be better than each other. We would not be concerned about whether we did the best in the class, but only about whether everyone was happy with what he or she was doing and how he and she was progressing. There would still be punishment, but these punishments would matter to the pupils. They would have to miss their favourite lessons for a week and have to take double lessons of their worst lessons instead.

We wouldn't be confined within walls of stone: we would go outside and experience the weather. We would travel and experience other pleasures. We would gain an understanding of the way of the world. Exams would be abolished, people would work together and alone, they would use other people's knowledge to enrich themselves and others would be the same with them. In my perfect school, there would be no bullies, there would be no insecurities. We would discuss our opinions in every lesson and everyone would listen and respect each other. Teachers and pupils would be equals, no privileges or disadvantages, everyone would be in the same boat. In my school, the only things they would ban would be unhappiness and pain, no room for lying, revenge and deceit.

But to have my perfect school, you need a perfect world, and if there were a perfect world, there would be no room for dreaming.

From this it's clear that how people behave one to another is crucially important. In Chapter 2 we have outlined the example that the head sets in talking – mainly positively of course – with all members of the community. The head models behaviour. If she shouts, other people will shout. If she is constantly finding fault, others will do the same. If she is optimistic, others will be too. As we have also noted earlier, the head is *skald* not scold.

The language used in school is also vital. It will reflect the real values the school stands for.

'Our language makes the school'

Language can make or break a school. Careless talk can sap a school's energy. The energy and motivation of even the most optimistic and willing colleagues can soon drain away. So, using 'we' rather than 'I' and 'you' is important, not simply in the spoken word but in written form too. You can use 'I' when taking the blame and 'you' rather than 'we' when giving praise and celebrating genuine success. It's here than the current buzzword 'personalization' comes in. Letters home, supposedly individual and personal, which refer to 'your son/daughter' and fail to mention names, are impersonal. Of course, general messages of information are different; but here too presentation is important. More than one successful headteacher has told me that the most important job they do is to write the weekly newsletter home, and how important it is to find the right words and tone.

'Non-teaching' staff is as offensive as it would be to refer to 'non-white' staff or pupils. It probably betrays a subliminal message about a hierarchy of the value put upon certain tasks and certain people in a bygone age. Continuing to use 'general ability' descriptors to describe 'brands' or 'streams' or referring to the 'bottom set' in their presence (or for that matter at all) is the modern equivalent to stamping 'remedial' on the inside cover of a book. It will encourage a misplaced notion of general ability, rather than the more generous multifaceted form to which a school may be saying it subscribes. Using 'learning' instead of 'work' is also a plus rather than a minus. (It's amazing what a difference it makes to refer to pupils getting on with their learning rather than work.)

The written language used in job-descriptions, the school prospectus, job advertisements, marking, school reports and staff handbooks is as vitally important as the spoken word in assemblies, tutorials, lessons, the corridors and the playground. All meetings are redolent with implied messages in what is said and in the body language of participants.

'In our school we sing from the same song-sheet': the elusive quest for consistency

This is the most intangible and elusive, yet vital, part of a school's success. It lies at the heart of what headteachers call 'consistency'. Clearly, the larger the school, the more important and tricky the issue becomes. After all, if you lay down too precisely what everyone must do, then individual flair and creativity will wither. Moreover, the most imaginative free-thinkers among the staff will soon seek new pastures. At the other extreme, where virtually anything goes, the school begins to fall apart. The smaller the school or department, the easier it is.

It's pushing the case but the more dysfunctional a school or department is, the more tightly the 'singing from the same song-sheet' rule needs to be drawn, agreed and – most vitally of all – followed by everyone. The more successful the school or department, the more leeway there is, not least for experimentation.

Are there things that are absolutely essential in 'singing from the same song-sheet'? We think that probably there are, and list below three practices that any school might feel will repay examination and debate. Each school, of course, will seek to ensure it hits the right note in its own particular version of the song staff are trying to sing together.

1 *Lessons*

Clearly, some agreement about the planning and recording of lesson plans is necessary. Whether it should be a three-, four- or five-part lesson will vary within and between departments, or indeed be laid down within descriptors of other possible models. But, for example, there will probably be agreement about 'greeting and seating'. That is to say the teacher is expected to be at the classroom door to allow students to go into the classroom to settle at their desks. Of course, there's a world of difference between carrying out that process well and doing it not so well. Do you stand between the open door and the opposite doorpost, increasing the likelihood of students brushing against you, while ignoring them as they enter, except to rebuke? Or do you spread the door open with welcoming arms, allowing maximum room and have a word with every student, perhaps beckoning a prospective troublemaker to whisper jocular threatening sweet nothings in his/her ear? Once inside, is there a convention that all staff, from the most to the least experienced, from the strongest to the weakest, set the seating-plan that suits them best? Is this ritual signalled across the whole school at year assemblies in the first week of each half-term?

2 *The corridors*

In one school, the students confessed to us that groups or gangs of students controlled the corridors. The school, of course, was dysfunctional except, as they observed, for the maths department, where a strong head of department had created an oasis of order. In another school, however, the conversations between staff and students in corridors, at break times and at the start and finish of the school day were pleasantly casual and frequent. So, conversation in corridors is an essential part of 'singing from the same song-sheet'.

Some minimal ground rules on display are another feature of corridor policy for departments/houses/stages. So, too, is agreement on the rapid retrieval of litter.

3 *Behaviour*

Unless there is consistency on expectations of behaviour, everyone in the school suffers. There is an American programme called 'Consistent Management Cooperative Discipline' (CMCD), which has been tried by some schools in challenging circumstances. All schools involved claim it is successful. When one describes the main features, they seem obvious. Teachers agree that when anyone wants silence they raise their hands and expect the pupils gradually, but rapidly, to do the same. The same practice continues in staff meetings. Every half-term, each member of staff – even the best – allocates their revised seating-plan for their lessons. Pupils are prepared for it at year assemblies by the head of year and the headteacher. Pupils apply for classroom jobs and are given them: one is to be the 'question monitor', involving using a beaker with all pupils' names on sticks and choosing one randomly whenever a teacher requires a respondent.

Primary schools will recognize the 'applying for classroom jobs' strategy. They will use 'circle time' and train pupil mediators. Both are to be found in secondary schools too, where the full array of peer tutors, peer counsellors and peer mentors reflect a structure that allows student involvement and student voice.

All schools mark out a preferred ratio of rewards to sanctions. All are carefully recorded, as are minor and major incidents, so they can be analysed and practice adjusted according.

'We listen and involve our pupils'

'Pupil voice' has been discussed as a desirable issue for many years. Pupils need a voice, however, that has consequences for the community. So, a school council without a budget is simply a 'talking shop'. Perhaps this extends to year councils in large schools.

Pupils are otherwise involved in different roles:

- Within the classroom in managing roles and in self-assessment as part of 'assessment for learning'.
- As peer tutors – an excellent way of learning and modifying behaviour for older pupils who are tasked to help younger ones.
- As peer mentors – within and beyond the classroom as a symbol of cooperative learning.
- As peer counsellors and mediators – to aid behaviour in and around school and act as a guard against bullying.
- As 'community workers' – helping locally as part of citizenship programmes.
- As editors and contributors to a pupil-produced magazine.
- As advisers on school design and buildings.

Pupils in the best schools are involved once a year in a 'student survey', which test the temperature of the school ethos and pupils' motivation to learn. The year council and school council receive written reports on the outcome.

Pupils are observers in the governing body and are involved in staff appointments.

Perhaps the best practice we have come across was in a junior school, which had what is called a 'headteacher for a day' scheme as part of 'children's day' each year. It involves six pupils from Year 6 putting themselves up as candidates for election two weeks before local elections and after SATs are over. Each has to publish manifestos and each has to attend a kind of hustings for questions and answers in front of staff and pupils. Voting takes place on local election day; all staff are eligible to vote, along with all pupils other than those who are late. The winner is announced and becomes 'headteacher for the day'. Aided by a cabinet of fellow pupils, she sets out proposals for the day for consultation with staff and pupils. The 'headteacher for the day' must take the 'praise assembly', when they give out 'achievement of the week' awards. She has tea with her favourite members of staff and prepares a newsletter for parents about her experience as headteacher. There is a fund-raising event. The day usually ends with a talent session.

'We have made our lunch-hour civilized and our lavatories pleasant places to visit'

For generations, school lavatories have been locked or are places where pupils visit only *in extremis*. (Children's bladders over the years have suffered in ways best left to the imagination.) It doesn't have to be like that. Some schools now see the lavatories as a touchstone of whether the improvements they've made are simply skin-deep. Involving what's called 'pupil voice', they suggest to the school's council issues that are concerning the 'school improvement group', seek their comments on the issues and ask about omissions. The school's council is then provided with a budget, either for the school or a part of the resources required to solve the particular project. The school's council can be guaranteed to raise issues that affect the environment. The lavatories are very likely to be on their list!

There are many solutions now claimed by schools. The best ingredients, apart from pupil involvement, in identifying solutions include refurbishment, installation of smoke detectors that only go off in the main office (so miscreants can be caught with a 'smoking gun' as it were) and then regular inspection of the toilets, either with paid attendants or regular patrols of school council members and staff of the school.

Lunch-hour

Chances are the school will also receive comment on the lunch-hour and the queues. Lunch-hours too can be transformed. Solutions range from condensing the lunch-hour to abolishing it altogether. The former can involve:

- Ensuring that all support staff have duties in their contract to help with supervision.
- Providing a rich range of activities, run either by the permanent staff, senior trained students with staff supervision or 'bought-in' entertainment.
- Having a clearly thought-through and implemented practice of music, used as 'choice' background with DJ – a rota of 'wannabe' students – during the lunch-hour or as background calming music to modify behaviour. (Certain music affects mood, and of course disposition to learn, in different ways.)
- Changing the nature of the playground. Here the pioneering work of 'Learning through landscapes' has meant that the conventional tarmacadam can be transformed into a varied sequence of spaces defined by plants, structures and sculpture.
- Welcoming student access to the carefully designed and well, supervised range of ICT facilities, including those in the library, where students can pursue their 'independent study' or 'homework' assignments.

The abolition of the lunch-hour has been implemented by a few schools. Anybody embarking on that option needs to visit a school that has done it and reflected on the outcome. Schools we know that have carried it out are the Compton in Barnet and Ninestiles in Birmingham. Each refurbished their dining area and catering facilities, a solution incidentally frequently pursued by those wishing to minimize queues. Then the two schools tackled the timetable, so students from different age groups (linked to faculty or subject) are off-timetabled at different times. For instance, between 11.45 a.m. and 1.30 p.m., groups have their lunch together in a setting of no more than 250. During their 'spare' time, after eating and while others are in learning, the students are encouraged to pursue studies or take part in supervised playground activity. Both schools report 'transformation': by choosing different age groups to eat together, they have minimized peer-group behaviour problems.

There are very few schools in challenging areas that would go back on their decision to have pre-school breakfast clubs. Opportunities include access for students and staff to morning papers and an environment calmed with appropriate background music.

All these measures – the lavatory refurbishment, the playground transformation, the use of music, the encouragement of access to pursue independent learning, the change in the lunch-hour, the start to the school day – minimize opportunities for bullying and reduce stress for staff. They are all part of creating an environment fit for learning. If music, food and water (always encouraged to be readily available in lessons to enhance concentration) are crucial, so also is the visual backdrop to learning. They are part of 'the way we do things here'. What now follows is a consideration of the 'visual' and the 'aural'.

What of the buildings and the visual environment?

We have already referred to the importance of the buildings themselves. Successful schools know there is even more to it than that and are conscious of the aural and spiritual environment. However, so many secondary schools apparently regard the school's surroundings as a distant afterthought and certainly do not give it the attention it deserves. In doing so they leave their school with at least a running sore.

Moreover, the natural inheritance, especially for teachers in secondary schools in the inner cities, is little short of horrendous. If they escaped the flimsy-system buildings of the 1960s, they were probably constructed out of disease-ridden concrete. Their windows will have been replaced as often as their flat roofs. So many also find their wiring and plumbing require renewal, disfiguring over and over again the daily environment of the teachers and students who pass each other in corridors where the frequently replaced cheap tiles have made the floor an unappealing patchwork quilt. Of course all schools receive different legacies from their authority's architects who originally designed them and those who have since sought to maintain them.

Consider the best of the independent sector. Students who attend Eton and Harrow are usually themselves from homes with fine surroundings, and not just architecturally: they are probably immersed in books and musical experiences from their first waking moments. Yet the surroundings they find themselves in at school take their breath away.

Some of the state sector can compare. I always thought that the legacy of Albert Smith, the architect of the old Oxfordshire and his mentor and counterpart in Buckinghamshire, Fred Pooley, would stand the test of time rather better than their counterparts in some of the other home counties. On the whole the rural inheritance of the Midlands and the North has bequeathed some splendid schools that would appear to have inhabited their surroundings for centuries. To make my point I describe two Oxfordshire schools in what was once the blanket-making town of Witney, just on the edge of the Cotswolds.

One school, Henry Box, is close to a beautiful church at the end of the green, surrounded by medieval houses. The school is a combination of the seventeenth, eighteenth and twentieth centuries. There are some buildings from the 1930s and a substantial extension from the 1960s and 1970s. The buildings are well spaced out and close to a tree-lined field. The school's inheritance would touch even the least visually aware child at some time during his career.

Wood Green is at the other end of town, a low, flat, grey, concrete-slabbed building of the 1950s with later additions, on the edge of a windswept green field. As it happens, a talented art teacher, ably assisted by a succession of perceptive leaders and committed colleagues, was keenly aware of this. The corridors were soon the subject of a year-round set of exhibitions and displays. They now are supplemented outside by gardens that would be on any 'open to the public' tour.

Why is it that children from the poorest backgrounds are given the worst surroundings and will the creation of academies and Building Schools for the Future (BSF) make this an outdated criticism? It used not to be so: the late Victorian schools and those before the Second World War, even afterwards, appeared to their contemporaries fine places, and in the 1950s, when the inner-city dwellers were moved to new estates, the general public called their new schools 'glass palaces'. The rot set in, often literally, during the 1970s in the wake of the oil crisis. Just at the time we became more generally aware of our environment and of the need to preserve and conserve we no longer needed new schools. And those we had, we regretted. Small wonder, therefore, that BSF has been so enthusiastically welcomed.

Case-study

The new headteacher of a school in a market town recognized immediately the subconscious influence of the monstrous design of the main building that people had lived with for 20 years. His first action was to plant climbers and creepers. His second was to pester the authority for the replacement of a flotilla of wooden-hutted buildings in the hope of a new block whose design might, with a bit of luck, have encouraged our architect to do something to improve the impact of the original building. For a whole generation of children at that school, the built environment suddenly became alive as the whole-school community devoted their attention to the school building project as it was designed and the whole environment improved.

Case-study

The headteacher of the 200-place primary school had been unhappy for two or three years with the generous, indeed overlarge playing fields. She persuaded the grounds maintenance team that their work would be less if half the field were left as a wild area. A goat was soon tethered in another part of the field and a dovecote appeared. Before long there were chicken and rabbit hutches and the whole community took their turn in looking after the animals. The children, of course, gained personal comfort from the animals and learned a lot about the cycle of life and the habits of various species. For some of it the start of a lifelong interest, for others a memorable interlude. In that school there really was no bullying.

Inside the school the *visual* environment is important. Here too primary schools have taught us much. For them it probably all started with the Cizec exhibition of children's art in Vienna in the 1930s, an event attended by a cluster of imaginative and influential HMIs led by John Blackie, who was later to be Senior Chief Primary Inspector. He recruited to his ranks the likes of Robin Tanner, a great artist in his own right, as well as a teacher.

As a result of their influence, there emerged a group of primary practitioners who were deeply convinced that artistic expression represented a rich vein of children's talent, which could be tapped very early when inhibition was less intrusive. Through successful experience in the various aspects of the arts, children's confidence would grow and therefore so too would their ability to master the basics such as reading, writing and numeracy, which our schooling system naturally emphasizes.

There is much in this argument, even if the release of artistic achievement at a young age often flatters to deceive so far as the talent is concerned. Nevertheless, what emerged was a few generations of primary teachers who gave ample rein to artistic expression. Through their training and their practice they learned the skills and techniques of good display.

It became the rule, therefore, rather than the exception, that the primary classroom and school itself has become a visual delight, even if it is sometimes now explicit in its purpose, so that secondary colleagues and a wider public tend to use the pejorative term 'decoration'. Yet look beyond the camouflage of the primary school and you can see its purpose. For example, the entrance foyer will illustrate various themes of the school curriculum or community activity. There will be evidence of practice in various media. In individual classrooms, it is as well to notice whether all the children's work is displayed.

Moreover, has the school avoided the trap of those early artistic enthusiasts of celebrating only art and literacy forms? Is there a mathematics puzzle or two? What of scientific work? And the successful primary school will occasionally turn the whole-school display activity for half a term to a linked theme, which supports a planned set of explorations of values to the whole school or community.

In the individual primary school classroom the environment is planned to encourage the child to autonomous learning: she should know where material, equipment and other learning resources are kept. Children need to take responsibility not only individually but collectively in the organization and conservation of resources. You will come across groups of pupils debating the work exhibited, and visiting parents will proudly be shown their own and their friends' efforts. Sometimes, in the best Foundation classrooms, the whole room will be transformed with huge models to some strange and exhilarating exhibit, which reinforces the children's learning from a visit (for example to a local coalmine, a farm or a theme park).

In the best-run primary schools, the school as a whole is a reflection of the individual classroom. At secondary schools such individual and whole-school environment polices are the exception rather than the rule. Why is that? First the primary teacher, through the Cizec–Blackie tradition, has been initiated into the importance of the visual in training, and almost all primary teachers have had longer training on average than their secondary colleagues. Most of them, with the exception of some in the expressive arts, have experienced hardly more than a passing mention of the techniques of display in their training. Second, of course, subject specialisms with their deep knowledge bias demand so much time and attention that the more general whole-school issues get lost. Moreover, secondary heads have for years come from that tradition, oblivious of their surroundings, as their studies so often testify.

It is, for example, still sadly rare to find the secondary headteacher's study wall deliberately exhibiting, on a rolling basis, examples of children's work: and where it happens it will so often be just art. We say 'just art' not because that is unimportant but because it shows that the head has not taken on board the much wider message of the question of display.

Case-study

One of us came across a London head two years ago who wistfully confessed he knew display was a really important whole-school issue but that after an initial push on his arrival it had deteriorated almost to its previous nonexistent level. He knew he had made the cardinal error of apportioning the job as one of two 'whole-school' responsibilities, to someone who had no credibility in the staffroom. Had a document been produced to explain the rationale for display? 'No!' Was the responsible member of staff initially invited to come up with short- and medium-term goals for display in certain areas of the school with criteria to guide choice? 'Well not really.' The questions and answers could have gone on: the real issue at stake, however, was not a judgemental review but a joining determination promoted by the head to revive the question of display. The head in question soon came up with the answer: he arranged for some of his staff from the English department to get together with local primary schools, all staffed by teachers skilled in display. In the second half of the summer term the best of the fourth-year junior work was jointly planned and displayed throughout the whole department, so that all the students in September could see something familiar. ⇨

He did not stop there; he used some teacher supply time to promote a debate about the quality of the English work before, during and after transition, with secondary colleagues having the pleasure of sharing their understanding of levels 3, 4 and 5. The next year the head managed to do the same for maths and found his English colleagues achieved the same outcome anyway.

In the meantime, two members of the English department had become skilled in display and an INSET day was planned, run entirely in-house by teachers who were known and respected as good teachers: they promoted more widely the issues of simple display, with a tactically chosen art colleague providing a workshop for staff members interested in becoming potters. (Interestingly they run that in their evenings.) The outcome of the day, therefore, was a staff leisure pottery club and a determination to mount a joint staff–pupil display of their wares in the hall before Christmas.

Finally 'workforce reform' provided the missing piece in the jigsaw. The school designated a member of the support staff to 'plan, organize and deliver' the visual environment. The person appointed found a ready-made set of knowledgeable improvement teams in each department.

The illustration tells not of the answer but of one that suited that head at that time with the staff he led. He seized on something – a primary–secondary transition – that was on the agenda anyway and simply fed in an idea to a group of enthusiasts. Already the school's environment is transformed for the better.

Case-study

In another secondary school, four years ago, an incoming head, with a couple of cheerful staff volunteers, transformed a desert of an entrance hall during a weekend. The children now gain experience in receiving visitors – a job strategically chosen for the third year. After all, if any one group of children are at risk of losing motivation it is Year 9. They look after the telephone too: it is all part of a carefully structured citizenship curriculum in Year 9 designed to find ways of capitalizing on their achievements, and part of an intensive review of their strengths and weaknesses, with extra teaching available to get them ready for the two years running up to GCSEs.

The same headteacher, a woman (it is significant that most visually aware heads in secondary schools tend to be women), soon tackled the visual environment systematically because she had that in mind – in the individual, informal 'get to know you' discussions that are a feature of all new headteachers in their first year.

From that she found she had a team of six members of staff across all departments, except science, who had expressed a keen interest in matters connected with environmental display or environmental teaching. Moreover, a cursory check of classrooms bore out their practice.

She invited them in for a chat one teatime and talked to them, first of their individual visions and then skilfully of what emerged as their collective vision but was, probably, hers all along. She promised to speak to the heads of faculties concerned, who were only too pleased to let their enthusiastic colleagues spread illustrations of their skills to the common areas of the faculties.

Already we have missed a step in the story – the science department. It was agreed that the probationary science teacher should be invited to be involved because there was no obvious person among the other members of staff. She was provided with extra INSET on the issue, as it happens from her partner who was a primary-trained teacher in a nearby school. The science team chose the topic for display and the probationer, along with some student teachers at the school, mounted it.

That is how it all started. Now, four years on, the school has students' work expertly displayed on three half-terms in the year. They have considered the checklist of questions set out towards the end of this chapter. All the staff (well, all but six old reprobates who claim they cannot learn new tricks but are being increasingly joked out of it) are involved in an end-of-session review of the work displayed.

We should add that the six reprobates now constitute a panel which gives an award to each department's efforts and explains the criteria they have used for the award. It was all jokey stuff at first, but it is not entirely that now. Again, the hard work involved has been powerfully assisted by the appointment of support staff as part of workforce reform.

What of the aural environment?

Somebody once said that with the echoing footsteps in the corridor, the shrill bells and the clanging doors, secondary schools can be confused with only one other sort of institution. Indeed, at the end of a school year, the cumulative effect of thousands of scraping chairs on hard floors, of dumped satchels, of banging doors and of lesson-change bells takes its toll on even the calmest teacher's patience.

In about 1971 Geoff Cooksey became the inspirational founding father of Stantonbury in Milton Keynes. He was preoccupied with carpets. Let us explain. At the time, I was an assistant education officer in Buckinghamshire. Among my duties was the design brief to architects for new schools and the liaison with a supplies officer colleague in the furnishing of them. Geoff Cooksey in Stantonbury presented an interesting challenge. We were both firmly convinced that schools should be flexibly designed to encourage teamwork but planned in a way that allowed quiet and individual teaching and learning. It seemed to us then a pity if the building were inflexibly constructed requiring teachers, through bricks and mortar, to work either as isolates or as teams. Very few architects have cracked that problem. At Stantonbury it was not such a problem because Roy Harding, the CEO at the time, recruited Geoff Cooksey from the schools council. He was unequivocally committed to teamwork and was also a charming, persuasive realist. The building exercise reflects an object lesson in planning and building a school effectively for present and future needs. What he wanted, however, was carpets.

This was 1972, remember, when we had just persuaded councillors that it was not a waste of money to supply carpet to quiet areas between pairs of primary classrooms and when the technology of industrially used carpets was in its infancy. Geoff wanted carpets everywhere. He got them in most places too.

The cleverer of the headteachers, incidentally, are linking the advent of carpets as a 'way in' on display in the particular departments affected by the carpeting. One of the unremarked benefits of Local Management of Schools is the feeling of power schools have enjoyed over the learning environment. They no longer feel guilty about leaving the decoration to an uncaring authority, but realize that it is their own priority.

So carpets are a contribution towards an aural strategy for a school and a powerful aid to better teacher–pupil relations and more effective learning and teaching. Let's consider some of the others.

I went into a Leicestershire school one wet lunchtime and couldn't believe what I saw. There at the milling area, close to entrance, the dining-hall and two main corridors, was a chamber orchestra running through its pieces. Half the dinner queue was watching and listening as though this were the most normal thing in the world. I asked one student in the queue if indeed this often happened. 'Yes', he said, 'but I prefer the jazz days – that's Thursdays.' He immediately became involved in an argument with another student in the queue who preferred the 'Asian days'.

We discovered a well-satisfied headteacher soon afterwards, who explained how the new head of music had decided that one way of unlocking the considerable musical interests of most students was to change their environment. For six weeks each term during lunch break, the students put on programmes of music that dominated the aural impression of the school's internal environment. The contrast in the other weeks was so stark that by popular request of the school council, the music teacher arranged for each form to play programmes of request in the same area – sufficiently moderated of course on the volume key not to become a nightmare.

Interestingly, the same school was debating the abolition of the electric bell system: they found it intrusive and were replacing it with a system of 'pagers' for teachers' pockets that were programmed to bleep for lesson-change time.

As we said at the beginning of this chapter, school climate is more than the aural or the visual. It is caught in the corridors, in the way people behave one to another, in doors that are held open or closed carelessly in your face, in adults and members of staff who have the time for a snatched smile or chat with passing students or pass unblinking or unrecognizing a fellow member of the community. How do schools establish that?

It comes from shared values, as a common agreement among teaching and support staff to concentrate on a few things and reinforce them come hell or high water. Mostly those things will be positive. They will affect the corridor and playground behaviour, the choice of prefects and their role (or the decision to have no prefects), the place for collective competition between groups rather than individuals and the celebration and honouring of excellence over a wide range of human talents. It will involve a close consideration of the service given by all members of the community, either within or to a wider community.

What few things a school says are important to students carry little weight if the staff's actions and everyday habits contradict them. The school that is concerned about this elusive and behavioural third dimension of the successful school's environment will examine carefully the messages conveyed by its rites, rituals and whole-school organization and practice. Some of the rites and rituals are illustrated in the stories of school life that punctuate the main chapters of this book, and some of the organizations and practices in the sections on leadership and maintaining success.

Summary

To summarize, we have some questions for those who would improve the school climate.

Personal and behavioural: the emotional aspect of schools:

1 Is there a code of conduct that applies to all members of the school community – students, staff, parents, governors?
2 How do our rites and rituals reflect that code of conduct and the school's principles, values or mission statement?
3 In what ways do we collect evidence with which we can review as objectively as possible the successes and shortfalls in personal standards of behaviour within the school community? Do we use student and staff surveys?
4 What elements of agreed 'singing from the same song-sheet' management practices have we in our school?
   • class rules agreed at the beginning of the school year and consistently upheld
   • pupils having jobs in class
   • changing class-lesson seating-plans every half-term
   • corridor pupil-traffic routes
   • entry to classrooms
   • 'assessment for learning' that is against personal previous best working and display
   • some agreed signal, universally observed by all in the community, for silence when someone wishes to speak.
5 How is the pupil voice expressed in the school?
   • a budget for the school council

- involvement of pupils in the appointment of staff process
- 'observers' on the governing body
- pupil peer-mentoring, tutoring, community service, counselling and mediating opportunities
- annual 'stakeholder' meeting.

Visual:

1 Who is responsible for display in the school and who else is involved? Do the pupils themselves have some responsibility in selecting and helping the display in communal areas?

2 Have we used 'artists in residence', perhaps from the local community or through the arts council, to engage youngsters in creating and celebrating something of beauty? For example, sculptures, murals, other artwork.

3 In secondary schools (where it is unlikely that more than a small proportion of staff have had training in display) how do new members of staff gain an understanding in display as part of their induction? How does this relate to the support staff designated under workforce reform to take responsibility for ensuring it happens?

4 When did we last use part of a professional development day to debate the visual impact of the school? How did we prepare for it? Did we use an outside or inside consultant to lead discussion within departments about display?

5 Within the classroom what are the walls used for? Are they used to display all the pupils' work? Are there some puzzles in the wall? How frequently are the displays changed? Is there some unfinished work to debate? In the secondary school does it reinforce the love of subject? Is it sometimes – say one half-term in two years – part of a deliberately planned whole-school cross-curricular survey? In the primary school does part of the work reinforce the school's language, maths and science policies, as well as perhaps the topic/theme of a group of classes?

6 Outside the school, who is responsible for the cultivated areas? How do we involve the older generation of the community in the maintenance and development of a part of the outside school? If our school is one sea of tarmacadam, how do we break that up? Are there seats for pupils, especially those not wishing to be swept along in informal team-games at break-time? Do the midday supervisors know and contribute to the development of the external environment? What INSET do we arrange for them?

7 In the staffrooms, are the notices cynical or humorous? Are there photocopied articles of interest on the noticeboard?

8 If our buildings are unremittingly unattractive, what can be done about it? Can the school be camouflaged by fast-growing creepers that don't damage the fabric? What is our strategy for ensuring that we don't become or remain the victims of vandalism?

Aural:

1 Are the corridors, even when empty, noisy? If so, what is the strategy for changing that? How much of the school is carpeted? What are the acoustics of the hall and dining area? What simple steps can be taken to make them better? Could, for example, the use of display materials help acoustically?

2 Is there a tannoy system in the school? If so, is it needed? Is the internal telephone bell intrusive to lessons and what other matters can be changed to decrease staff stress? What about the tables and chairs? Do doors naturally slam?

3 Is there a thought-out policy of music for dinner-times and for the social areas for breaks before and after school? Is there a mix of pop, jazz, reggae, eastern and western classical music? Is some of it student-performed and some reproduced? If there needs to be a bell to summon students from the field, does it need to be institutional?

The new learning and communication technologies:

1 Is there access before and after school for students to use computer facilities?

2 Have we used to the full the potential of our e-learning platform to personalize learning?

3 How do we use digital display in the classroom and public areas?

It's easy to overlook or become complacent about the environment and school climate: in the end it can be taken for granted. Everyday practices in behaviour, in particular, can slip without constant reinforcement.

We don't know of an outstanding school that doesn't continually seek to make small improvements to its aural, visual and behavioural surroundings.

6 Partnerships and stakeholders

A school is not an engineering model; it is a city state with citizens, with passions and factions, dreams and fears. If it can become a vital, open, learning community what a message it has to offer to a wider world.

David Clark (1996)

The best case for public education has always been that it is a common good. Everyone, ultimately, has a stake in the calibre of schools, and education is everyone's business.

Michael Fullan (2004)

Partnerships are the key to success

As we have seen, the good school will continue to achieve success through developing leadership at all levels, focusing on the core business of learning, teaching and assessment, and of sustaining improvement through professional development and innovation. However, there can be a disproportionate influence of factors outside school on children and young people's achievement, and in order to sustain success schools must connect to their community, seeking out new forms of social capital. Further, the *Every Child Matters* agenda demands multi-agency and partnership working, as no school can deliver this on its own. Partnership working is the key to success, with reference to children and young people being healthy, staying safe, making a positive contribution, achieving economic well-being and enjoying and achieving. When questioned, children and young people often highlight safety at school, home and in public places as a key concern – safer school partnerships can provide the security the child needs to excel. Drop-in clinics at children's centres place schools at the heart of the community and boost both pupils' health and attainment levels, with healthy eating and walk-to-school schemes playing their part. Many schools seek to achieve the 'healthy schools' standards through a range of school and community activities. In terms of economic well-being, there are a wide range of organizations, services and business through which students can gain a greater economic understanding and an awareness of the world of work apart from through the curriculum. Businesses can contribute support, in terms of both skilled and committed employees and of sponsorship, as in support for specialist colleges. Some schools are linked to businesses which provide mentors for students. Other business volunteers help schools with their Young Enterprise programmes and work through Education Business partnerships. The challenges of 'making a positive contribution' to the community demands that the school's citizenship programme is well taught, with a developed understanding of students' rights and responsibilities and those of others, and taking an active part in community activities such as environmental projects, local charities and local regeneration.

Partnerships may be defined as 'a sense of community created across social systems' and are at their strongest when they are established and maintained through the learning process as a process of community education. School leaders are pivotal in partnerships in the community that centre on children because the school is often the institution that all the adults recognize as important in their lives. Therefore, practitioners and school leaders need to engage a range of stakeholders and partnerships actively and consistently over time through talking to the community, knowing and understanding its needs and expectations and planning how the school can contribute to meeting these requirements. This is a two-way process and in many instances the community is a wider source of untapped skills and resources that can also support the school in its particular aims and objectives. Good schools model effective behaviours that will support successful partnerships, including time and energy, showing commitment, respect and trust. More than ever they are aware of their role in the community outside school, their relationship with community leaders and with parents, and the need to distribute leadership and to communicate effectively with other professionals.

So who are the stakeholders? The pupils and their parents have the greatest stake as the school primarily exists for them as a public service. Other stakeholders include staff, governors, community leaders and organizations. Pupils have the principal claim to attention, and the literature of school improvement and effectiveness is replete with strategies to involve them in decisions about their work and the running of the school – something we deal with in Chapter 5 and elsewhere. Parents and governors are referred to separately in this chapter. Often support staff, rather than teaching staff, are more likely to live and work in the vicinity of the school and have their children attend the school. We accept that this is not invariably the case; we are just making the point that the investment of someone working in the school and living close by (certainly if they are a parent too) is greater than that of someone living in a different community altogether. Moreover, the wise school realizes that the most powerful messages from adults about a school get carried through the local community by those who work and learn there. Thus the school's teaching and learning assistants, midday supervisors, school-meal staff, caretakers, administrative staff, technicians and learning mentors are more likely to carry the reputation of the school than teachers and senior leaders of learning. This, of course, has all sorts of implications for staff development as a key process and provision that is made for the school workforce more widely. We also have to recognize that according to the school's context, stakeholders bring more or less capacity to their task. The nearer a school is to poverty, the less likely it is that these students' backgrounds will have the sense of consistent support that gives any student and the school they attend a head start in unlocking talent and potential. It is as though the stakeholders in such a situation are more loosely and less permanently coupled to the school's purpose: indeed, in such situations turbulence and mobility of students and the community is a daily reality. These schools require energy, drive, skill and enthusiasm to a disproportionate degree as they sustain an unrelenting press to deliver the five outcomes of *Every Child Matters*. They will need even more effective partnerships with parents, social care and health services, with other local schools and community organizations.

Whatever their local circumstances, all schools are expected to offer extended services to their community by 2010 and many schools have now been officially designated as 'extended schools'. An extended school, apart from its duty to orchestrate before- and after-school clubs and care opportunities, can offer an integrated service for children, working across professional boundaries to raise standards – including prevention and early intervention and better support for parents and families. The core offer includes study-support activities, high-quality childcare, parenting support, swift and easy referral to specialist support services and community access to ICT, sports and arts facilities.

By building rich and purposeful relationships with parents, communities and local agencies where learning runs in both directions, schools can build and communicate successful approaches to achievement. Schools can also appeal to the increasing rates of volunteerism and community commitment among adults. However, connecting to the outside rarely means easy consensus, but something that requires openness of mind and determination.

Parents and carers

Parents make a difference. A review by Professor Charles Desforges (2003) found that parents can positively influence their children's learning by providing:

- a secure and stable environment
- intellectual stimulation through play and curiosity
- parent–child discussions
- good models of social and educational values
- high aspirations relating to good citizenship and personal fulfilment.

There is compelling evidence that parental aspirations, expectations and involvement have a major impact on children's attainment. Parents also have an impact where they have contact with schools to share information, and where they participate in school events, the work of the school and in school governance.

Good schools think strategically about the ways in which they can involve parents more and more deeply in supporting their children's learning. Good practice in Early Years has led the way in working with parents as assets and as partners in their children's learning and growth. Workshops and discussion groups, at which parents can see and understand how children are learning in different areas of the curriculum, can help them to gain access.

Of course involving parents can be socially complex, especially in areas of high deprivation or where children are vulnerable. In these situations schools will draw upon good partnerships with other agencies such as social services, youth-offending teams or voluntary organizations. However, there should be a common core of building trust with parents, establishing a dialogue about their children's learning and providing information on what they can expect from school and the progress their child is making.

Beyond this universal provision, good schools have thought through where more focused energy may be necessary, particularly for families with specific additional needs and where parents may be hostile to involvement with the school. Particular attention is required to deal with the needs of children in care, which ought to be the school's top priority.

Key features of effective work with parents

- Accessible literature covering what all parents want to know about the school, which also includes a website and regular newsletters.
- Information being made available to parents on what they can expect from school regarding individual pupils' progress. This ideally and increasingly includes access to lesson-plans and learning materials.
- Frequent communication, telling parents clearly how their children are doing but also about the variety of learning events that they can attend.
- Mechanisms for parents to give feedback on the quality of education, for example through regular surveys of parental satisfaction, which of course should feed into the school evaluation form.
- Home–school contracts to support learning at home in cooperation with the school, which may involve particular partnership schemes such as home–school planners, home–school reading diaries, sending books or work home, lending libraries for toys and books for younger pupils or homework diaries for older pupils. In this sense parents are not only involved with the school but demands are made of them to contribute to their children's learning.
- Regular consultation and review sessions with the parents and also with students – particularly in secondary schools. Students can review their work with the form tutor and their parents and agree targets for further progress. Many schools, through 'achievement days', are now

encouraging the student rather than the form tutor to lead the review, thereby taking full ownership of the issues.

- A termly class meeting in primary schools to explain to parents the nature of the coming term's curriculum and how parents can reinforce this at home (backed up by resource materials).
- Thematic parents' evenings or open weeks around such topics as the teaching of reading and numeracy or the use of ICT, at which parents can understand and participate in the learning process and support their children appropriately. Some schools invite parents to work alongside their children in a particular subject area.
- Opportunities provided by the school for parents to enhance their own learning, sometimes gaining 'access' qualifications, for example communication skills, parenting skills, health and safety education and information technology. In primary schools in particular there may be a parents' room or base that can be used for a variety of activities and courses.
- Celebrating success through exhibitions, class assemblies, display of pupils' achievements and performances in music, dance, drama and sport.
- Parents and community members becoming involved in the teaching and learning process as learning assistants (volunteers or formally employed), working alongside teachers or taking up other functions within the school.

The effort to draw in parents in terms of establishing meaningful partnerships can be considerable, but the prize is great. Good schools think through the style and tone of contacts that are set in the first place by the head and senior leaders. However, essential to success is the consistency with which they are maintained by all staff. Consistency of approach to pupils' work and behaviour also makes a strong contribution to the home–school partnership. Parents need to feel that the school is a community of place for them with welcoming signs and easy access. Above all, parents should feel welcome in the school and be actively encouraged to participate in the life of the school through informed contacts, social events, as volunteers in classroom and through lots of intervention with the work their children take back and forth between home and school. Parental views are now often sought both informally and formally through questionnaires, as schools are anxious to demonstrate their knowledge of stakeholder views generally to bolster the process of self-evaluation. Good schools will make sure that they take parents' views seriously and act upon them.

Parents in partnership – support at transition from primary to secondary school:
- DVD for parents on supporting their children.
- Use of peer-parent volunteers.
- September programme of courses on supporting your child in the secondary school, led by facilitators.
- Weekend residentials for particular families as part of extended school provision.
- Specific curriculum workshops focusing on Key Stage 2 to Key Stage 3 continuity in English and maths.

Governors

The relationship of the governing body and a whole school, with the head, other staff and parents is the most unresearched part of school effectiveness and improvement. Governors have been given a much more powerful position of influence in the school system since the mid 1980s. They now have many powers that were formerly exercised by the local authority (LA).

In our experience, at any one time there will be 1 or 2 per cent of school governing bodies that are at loggerheads with the head and/or some other part of the school's management. Certainly, headteachers who are losing their grip will seek either to magnify the governing body (in order to bolster their position) or to keep the governing body in the dark (in order to 'keep the lid' on the situation). The position of staff governors when things go wrong is extremely difficult.

As we have said, such cases amount to no more than 1 or 2 per cent. In the main, the relationship between the head and the governors is not problematic: perhaps the key in this is to help and encourage governors when things are going well so that their work in its own right can sustain improvement.

Unlike other stakeholders, governors represent not only themselves but also a constituent group such as parents, staff, the LA or the community. They particularly need to work hard at being the 'critical friend' to the head and the staff: this requires them to be known in the school, since otherwise their questions will be seen as hostile or irrelevant.

Governing bodies now have four main tasks:

1 To provide a strategic view of where the school is heading and help to decide the school's strategy for improvement so that its pupils learn most effectively and achieve the highest standards.
2 To monitor and evaluate educational standards and the quality of education provided, asking challenging questions and pressing for improvement.
3 To assume direct responsibility for oversight of financial management, the recruitment of senior staff and some disciplinary matters.
4 To act as critical friend to a school, providing the headteacher and staff with support, advice and information, drawing on members' knowledge and experience.

In carrying out these targets there needs to be a clear understanding by governors and heads of the difference between management and governance. In practice, most governing bodies work through a series of processes and find themselves to a greater or lesser extent 'advising', 'steering', 'mediating', 'supporting' and 'holding the school to account'. While each governing body will decide for itself *how* it should be involved in the running of a school, like all other partners it should demonstrate a commitment to continuous improvement, both in terms of improving the quality of education for the pupils and also in developing its own learning capacity and that of most of the whole-school community. This will mean establishing a climate in which there is open discussion among governors, the head, staff, parents and, in outstanding schools, sometimes students, to ensure that there is a shared, common language about roles and responsibilities. As so often in school improvement, the process is the key. Governors also have a vital role in policy-making, development-planning, and monitoring and evaluation, and will wish to be informed and inform themselves about a school's strengths and weaknesses so that they can work effectively with the head and staff in particular.

Governors and development-planning

Governors can participate fully in development-planning if a development-planning day for all governors is set aside each year, well in advance. On a development-planning day governors work alongside staff in conducting an audit and setting targets (both general and for pupil attainment) for next year's school development plan. The subsequent monitoring of the plan can be helped by giving each subcommittee responsibility for reporting on a key element of the plan. A similar process is necessary when discussing the school evaluation form (SEF). The more governors, like staff, that can be involved in planning and review, the better the outcome.

Progress reports

The schedule for governing body meetings needs a rolling programme of progress reports. These can cover the work of individual subject departments in the secondary school and particular curriculum areas in the primary school, in addition to other aspects such as behaviour and attendance, ideally including both quantifiable and quantitative data. It is also useful to discuss the structure of the headteacher's termly report with the head, so that it enables regular review by all the governing body.

Assigned governors

In some places specific governors are successfully linked to a phase/aspect of curriculum leaders in primary and special schools, and to heads of department in secondary schools. These governors 'champion' particular areas and take a direct interest in pedagogy, resources and achievement. They are well placed to help prepare and receive reports to the governing body. Already a 'responsible' governor has a statutory role related to special educational needs in the school, working closely with the special educational needs coordinator (SENCO). However, this concept could be widened considerably. Other examples would be a governor given prime responsibility for equal opportunities issues or, similarly, health and safety. Whatever the link role, it is important to draw up a short job-description so that everybody is clear about their role.

Governor visits

It is true to say that governors who do not visit the school during the working day will always struggle to have credibility in the school community. Visits, moreover, give governors the chance to evaluate the impact of their plans and policies on the day-to-day operation of the school. However, it is important to have a visiting policy, with a code of practice negotiated with the staff, which lays down the different set of circumstances and occasions for visits and criteria for whether there are to be written outcomes reported back to the governing body. Misunderstanding about the purpose of visits is widespread in our experience, especially when they are in the planning stage.

Rotation of governor meetings

When governing body meetings are held in different classrooms or areas of the school, and when each meeting begins with a short presentation from the 'host' staff about specific curriculum, teaching and learning issues, the focus of the governors' discussion is being set. For example, a governing body that meets in the nursery/Reception area in one school we know has a way of engaging in debate about the quality of provision in the Early Years, baseline assessment, links with parents and other related issues. Similarly, a governing body that meets in the arts faculty of a secondary school, and as part of its agenda considers more fully the resourcing and provisions of the arts curriculum, will persuade the arts faculty that it is taking the faculty's concerns seriously. Such meetings can only be 'tasters' before other governing body business, but they add considerably to the knowledge and capacity of governing bodies to make key decisions and, if the host staff stay as observers, facilitate good and informed relations between staff and governors.

Governors' communications

Governors need to be 'visible', in the sense that if they are to be the body that is accountable for the school the pupils, the parents, the staff and a wider community need to know of their work and their role. All the usual media will need to be considered to ensure that this happens. These will include newsletters, displaying photographs of the governors in school along with the rest of the staff, regular open sessions or 'surgeries' and participation in school events. Working on specific subcommittees or joint task groups with other partners in the school provides another opportunity for governors to be more widely known. Subcommittees such as finance and resources, premises, personnel and curriculum can help concentrate expertise to the benefit of the school, but specific task groups can also be useful in building effective partnerships with teaching staff, parents and the local community in the production of joint reports to all governors.

Governors' induction and training

Those schools that take governors seriously allocate mentors and provide induction packs and briefings. New and existing governors need key documentation such as existing policies and plans, reports on the school, pupil-performance data and basic administration information. Mentors are usually other governors, but having additional mentoring from a member of staff is also very beneficial. Training and accrediting learning for governors is usually arranged through specifically designed programmes, often from the governor-training unit of an LA but sometimes through higher education. Governors are entitled to access to training and, like all learners, need to be encouraged and valued, so why not certificate specific training experience, either in the school or at a local centre? Training in topics such as understanding school performance data and target-setting, monitoring and evaluation, financial management and personnel issues are the logical steps in developing the governor's role in improving schools.

Celebrating success

Celebrating success can be overlooked unless it is carefully planned in the routine of the school. This may consist of the involvement of a rota of governors in the weekly awards assembly or participation in enriched extracurricular activities such as the performing arts, sport, clubs and societies, residential experiences or celebrating a successful Ofsted report. Certainly, all governors need to be involved in some of the range of experiences and activities provided by the school so that they can feel they are part of a celebrating, as well as an improving, community of learners. They may often be used to present certificates and commendations, but it is important that governors themselves are valued for their contribution, through the imaginative use of awards for significant service.

Good partnerships with governors are essential if school improvement is to be sustained. Governing bodies have a vital role in establishing a collaborative culture that encompasses staff, pupils, parents and the wider community. Governors can make schools better by shaping and guarding the values and vision of the school through its key roles of strategic planning and monitoring and evaluation.

> The key characteristic of the effective governing body is its ability to understand and implement the distinctive contribution it can make to the management of the school.
>
> Nigel Gann (1998)

Business

If the greater involvement of parents with schools has been impressive in the last few years, then that of business has been equally striking. Education Business Partnerships have played an important part in connecting the learning that young people undertake in schools to the world of work outside. One of the *Every Child Matters* outcomes relates to achieving economic well-being, and local business are increasingly playing their part in working closely with school in explaining and exemplifying the world of work. School business partnerships are being promoted in many different ways and good schools are seizing all the opportunities presented to them. They are seeking to develop learning for work that goes beyond work experience and careers guidance towards a more structured form of workplace learning, in which students learn through direct experience, but relate that experience to learning outcomes that are connected to their goals for personal development and to their accredited school-based learning. Workplace learning is factored into the curriculum as part of a range of course options, and placements are seen as part of a student's long-term education development rather than just a short burst of context specific experience. As a result of deeper local partnerships with business employers, teachers, support staff and students become more focused and motivated. The so-called 'work-related curriculum' is providing an increasing range of vocational qualifications in the 14–19 phase and new diplomas will be on offer by September 2008.

The Department of Children, Schools and Families has reaffirmed the importance of every secondary school, particularly in forming links with business organizations. Many schools already have a direct partnership with a business, via sponsorship of their specialist status, through which they have sought to provide extra learning and training opportunities. Other schools have sought business support in developing their programme of out-of-hours learning, enterprise education and financial literacy.

Critical friends

This brings us to the question of a school's need for 'critical friends'. Under the New Relationship with Schools all schools have been allocated a school improvement partner (SIP) to formally carry out this role, but there are other visitors to the school who can contribute to the school's success by assuming part of this role. They are either commissioned by the school, such as consultant leaders, education consultants, researchers, university staff and business partners, or visiting on behalf of statutory agencies, such as health and social care professionals and, of course, Ofsted, which may be inspecting particular aspects of the curriculum as well as a formal inspection. The LA and diocese should also act as critical friends to help the school reflect on its progress and open up further opportunities.

> He has the right to criticise who has the heart to help.
>
> Abraham Lincoln, quoted in F. Sennett (2004)

Of course, the term 'critical friendship' can mean different things to different people and at its worst lapse into 'unfriendly criticism' or 'uncritical friendship'. 'Hostile witnesses' bring to their involvement in the life of a school a bias towards negativity that is at once condemnatory. Perhaps more dangerous, because it is seductive, are 'the uncritical lovers' who are so besotted with what they perceive as the all-embracing success of the school that they tend to devalue the currency of praise because all their comments are positive and offer no suggestions for further improvement. Successful schools usually have critical friends who understand and are sympathetic to the purposes of the school, know its circumstances very well and are skilled in offering a second opinion (or sometimes a first opinion) about an issue only half-perceived by the school itself, or if perceived, seen as impenetrable.

To a greater or lesser extent critical friends:

- ask questions which are increasingly focused, but speculative not judgemental
- use 'we' and 'you' (but not 'I' except to promise or take blame) in equal measure
- when giving a view leave questions or sentences half-finished to preserve dignity
- identify personally with a school's success and its failures
- enable the school to carry out internal self-evaluation better
- see strengths as well as points for development
- balance 'appreciative enquiry' with 'problem-solving'.

Critical friends are invaluable to schools and almost all case-studies in school improvement research refer to people who are clearly in that role. A school needs a range of partners and critical friends for different aspects of school life. Each critical friend needs a precise and focused specialism, but also some peripheral vision in order to be sure that they are building levels of energy (perhaps through appreciative enquiry). In such a way they look at subjects and areas of curriculum experience, perhaps through the National Strategies local consultants, attendance and behaviour, outcomes from *Every Child Matters*, extended school provision and relationships with the local community. Their analysis of the current situation, their questions and development points can be reflected in the School Evaluation Form and the School Development Plan and make a considerable contribution to the momentum of school improvement.

The school improvement partner

Of all the partners and critical friends it is the school improvement partner that acts as formal critical professional friend to the school, helping its leadership to evaluate its performance, identify priorities for improvement and plan effective change. The role is to build the school's capacity to improve the attainment of pupils and to achieve other key outcomes for pupils that bear on achievement. The SIP acts for the school's maintaining authority and is the main (but not the only) conduit for LA communication with the school. At the time of writing, the system is relatively new, but schools are quickly learning how to make the relationship work effectively. For most schools the SIP is another headteacher, who offers a reality check as well as professional challenge and support. Getting that balance right is key so that the school feels the practice is improved by interactions with the SIP and there is evidence of impact. The SIP's focus on pupil progress and achievement, and the many factors that influence it, including pupil well-being, extended services and parental involvement, can be of great assistance to the school's self-evaluation process and key priorities and targets for improvement.

Since a school's governing body is responsible for the strategic direction of the school, the SIP needs to interact with the governing body as well as offering the headteacher a professional view on the overall direction of the school. The SIP also has specific responsibility for advising governors on the headteacher's own and the school's collective performance-management arrangements.

As the name implies, school improvement partners are the crucial partners in school improvement with a line of accountability to the LA. Good schools use the school improvement partners, along with a range of other critical friends, to help them lead and manage school improvement.

We have tried in this chapter to reflect on the importance of climate setting and the school's need for critical friends. The contribution of stakeholders and partners to school improvement is best done through appreciative enquiry, building on existing strengths through a process of collective review. As critical friends, LAs, parents, governors and other partners are invaluable to schools, in that they ask focused questions such as 'How well are we doing?', 'How do we compare with similar schools?', 'What more should we achieve?', 'What must we do to make it happen?' Stakeholders and partners need to strike a careful balance between pressure and support. If they can do this, working with each other, there will be an increased likelihood of success.

The road to school improvement is always under construction.

Anon.

7 Reviewing for success: collective review and school self-evaluation

It is an index of the nation's health when its school communities have a high level of intelligence and know how to use the tools of self-evaluation and self-improvement.

John MacBeath (1999)

I keep six honest serving men,
(they taught me all I know),
Their names are what and why and when
and how and where and who.

Rudyard Kipling (1902)

In the spirit of Kipling's quotation we should first ask the question 'Why should schools engage in self-evaluation?' and then move on to the 'what' and 'how' and 'who'.

The 'why'

Good schools engage in self-evaluation because it helps them improve even more, not just because it is demanded through the School Evaluation Form and the Ofsted inspection process. They practise intelligent accountability founded on their own views of how they are serving their learners. In order to offer the best possible education for learners, staff and governors are constantly evaluating how well the school provides for them, the impact of this provision and how it can be improved. From this self-evaluation process arise the key priorities for improvement and a single, integrated development plan that maps out the actions needed to bring about improvement.

The striking characteristic of the 'moving' school as opposed to the 'stuck' school is that it has a culture that sustains critical reflection and enquiry, coupled with a determination to secure continuous improvement. Rigorous self-evaluation is the dynamic of school improvement. It is not undertaken for the

If one does not know to which port one is sailing, no wind is favourable.

Seneca

purpose of inspection but is integral to the school improvement process and the highest common denominator of shared values. Successful schools have a very high consensus about their values captured in their mission statements and reinforced consistently at every opportunity. In these schools there is high commitment, cohesiveness and collaboration that reinforces and thrives on intellectual curiosity and a willingness to be imaginative. There is a will to collect evidence and debate implications. In such a thriving self-evaluation culture there will be supportive and knowledgeable leadership, an openness to improvement, honesty and trust, reflective dialogue, good collaboration and accepted norms of sharing, a relentless focus on student learning and a celebration of cutting-edge practice. In short, the school is a professional learning community that builds in time for collective enquiry and review where staff are encouraged to collaborate by learning with and from each other. The school itself is organized as a learning community that travels forward, promoting a dialogue for new knowledge, thinking and practice.

A self-evaluating school never thinks it has arrived: it is always on a journey towards new heights of excellence.

The 'what'

The criteria set out in Ofsted's evaluation schedule and the questions in the SEF are very helpful when carrying out school self-evaluation, although it is worth emphasizing here that completing the SEF is not, in itself, self-evaluation but only the place to record and summarize the findings of a thorough self-evaluation process.

Schools should evaluate all they do, but not necessarily all at once, something that we will return to under the 'how' section.

In terms of 'achievement' and 'standards', schools need to know how well learners perform in terms of

- the overall standards they attain;
- the standards achieved by different groups such as girls and boys, those from different ethnic groups, those with different special needs, those eligible for free school meals, the gifted and talented, those children in public care;
- the progress made by individual pupils and different groups of learners over time, particularly across all the Key Stages.

All this will involve the reviews and analysis of achievement data to examine critically trends, patterns and anomalies so that informed priorities and targets can be established. With regard to learners' 'personal development' and 'well-being', it is the extent to which they are meeting the *Every Child Matters* targets that is the test of:

- being healthy

- staying safe
- enjoying and achieving
- making a positive contribution
- achieving economic well-being.

It is much harder to quantify learners' personal development than academic achievement, but good schools have developed both quantitative and qualitative indicators that give them a range of evidence on which to make a secure judgement about current provision and future priorities. Evaluation about the quality of provision will include the quality of teaching and learning and a judgement on how well teaching meets individuals' needs, as well as the suitability and rigour of assessment. It will also include evaluation of the curriculum offered and how this, and other activities, meets the range of needs and interests of learners as well as how well learners are guided and supported. Good schools will have already evaluated the above in terms of their provision of personalized learning and its key components of effective teaching and learning strategies, assessment for learning, curriculum entitlement and choice, school organization and strong partnerships beyond the school, and established some key priorities.

The quality of leadership and management throughout the school is often the most difficult area for heads, senior staff and governors to make a judgement on, and often an external perspective can be useful in this exercise. Certainly it is crucial that any evaluation takes account of impact in terms of the outcome for learners and the quality of provision, as well as setting a clear direction for the school, leading to improvement and effectively monitoring overall performance.

In terms of overall effectiveness and efficiency, governors and staff will need to evaluate the plans they have implemented, any strategies for improvement, whether resources are being effectively used and, in particular, the impact of action taken on the learning and well-being of the school's learners. The relationships a school develops with external agencies, such as the links between the school and other providers, services, employers and organizations, are also important. Crucially they will be concerned to judge the capacity of the school to make future improvements. Good schools are able to do this by demonstrating the effectiveness of their self-evaluation processes, identifying how well the school serves its learners, the integration of self-evaluation into their key management systems, and the link between self-evaluation and actions to achieve the school's longer-term goals for development, most notably demonstrated in a high-quality, integrated improvement plan.

In all these aspects of a school's work there are whole sets of progress and performance indicators to consider, some of which can be measured and benchmarked against the performance of similar schools. However, the successful, self-evaluating school knows how to go further than this. It asks questions about more difficult areas, such as the extent to which proclaimed values are really shared in the school community, the quality of relationships and common caring, the effectiveness of communications, indeed the entire ethos and culture of the school. Under the 'what' of school self-evaluation it is possible to miss the mindset and reality of school life, sometimes expressed simply as 'the way we do things around here'. Good schools are very aware of what makes up their school culture, the 'glue' that holds everyone together, and how this can be seen as a positive development force. However, although they may believe that the most important aspects of the culture are now embedded, they never take this for granted and are constantly assessing whether their culture is developing, stagnating or declining and if necessary refreshing the values and the vision that made it such a good school in the first place. It is, of course, much more difficult to evaluate such community qualities as cohesiveness, commitment and collaboration, but we should always ask the question 'Is this a happy school?'

> Not everything that can be counted counts and not everything that counts can be counted.
>
> **Albert Einstein (1950)**

The 'how'

So far we have established the 'why' and 'what' school of self-evaluation, but 'how' do good schools evaluate the quality of their provision and 'who' is involved in this process? Here there is no set Ofsted model, but the best schools have simple, yet well-understood and consistent processes to evaluate progress in practical ways through their day-to-day work. They know that good self-evaluation is based on a wide range of telling evidence rather than assertion and anecdote. They will collect, analyse and evaluate evidence by

> Collective review is ensuring that the sum of the parts are exceeded by the collective whole.
>
> **Tim Brighouse and David Woods (1999)**

- examining current attainment data and trends over time.;
- tracking the results of each pupil's progress and attainment;
- benchmarking data with similar schools on attainment, staffing, finance, attendance and exclusions;
- evaluating the quality of learners' personal development and the impact of external services on the learning and well-being of learners;
- observing and evaluating teaching on a regular programme;
- gathering learners', parents', teachers' and other stakeholders' views and perceptions about the quality of the school's provision;
- using the results of internal monitoring undertaken by review groups, senior staff or governors;
- consulting external reports and views from the wider school community and external agencies such as the LA, feeder schools and other providers, as well as a range of critical friends;
- engaging in dialogue with the SIP in validating the processes used by the school in carrying out self-evaluation and the outcomes that result from this;
- working with governors to monitor and evaluate the standards and quality of education provided, drawing on their knowledge and experience.

Most schools will use tools such as questionnaires for pupil and parent views, interviews, minutes of meetings, data analysis and externally commissioned reports on different aspects of provision to complement their existing self-evaluation systems. However, the best schools will go further and deeper than this, gaining insights from a range of reflective dialogue at every level of the school such as student consultations, 'learning threes' for evaluating teaching and learning (mutual observation and third-party moderation), action research groups, focus groups, coaching and mentoring. Schools like this involve everybody in the process of continuous self-review, not as an onerous chore or because an Ofsted inspection is due but as part of the rhythm of everyday school life. They have developed what has been called 'enquiry-mindedness' – actively searching for understanding and using systematic enquiry procedures to stand back and think about their schools.

At its best the whole-school community speaks the language and experiences the process of self-evaluation as an integral part of existing management systems such as the performance management of staff, continuous professional development, assessment and target-setting for learners' academic and personal development, reporting to governors, as well as the usual cycle of planning and review where everybody participates. It is very important that the school has an agreed cycle of self-evaluation as part of its continuous drive for improvement. Although good schools will have embedded systems of review in all activities, the rhythm and pace of whole-school review keeping the SEF as a living, changing document, will also be planned thoroughly. Schools have now developed annual self-evaluation timeline plans making sure that they cover all aspects of the school's work such as performance data, the quality of teaching and learning, *Every Child Matters* outcomes, and the organization and management of the school. They plan ahead the opportunities formally to sample stakeholders' and pupils' views, as well as lesson observations and work scrutinies.

> The real voyage of discovery consists, not in seeking new landscapes, but in having new eyes.
>
> Marcel Proust

There are, of course, many approaches and combinations of approaches to effective school self-evaluation, but good schools will usually combine the following approaches to give them the best of insight and establish priorities for further improvement:

- **The stakeholder approach** – which involves the school in surveying the views and attitudes towards the school of pupils, parents, staff and the wider community. Ofsted asks how the school gathers views and how often, what the views are and what action the school has taken in response to the views. There are now a range of 'objective' questionnaires especially for pupils and parents that schools can use. Some of them are capable of being analysed and compared to responses from other schools, but smart schools will also use ongoing approaches to sampling stakeholder views such as parent and learners' review days or evenings, evaluation of INSET days and activities, the views of employers concerning work experience or making aspects of school self-evaluation part of the citizenship curriculum.

Whatever and wherever the views of stakeholders are gained it is essential to demonstrate what difference this has made.

- **The checklist/audit approach** – where a school carries out an audit against a list of questions generated either by the school, LA, DfES, Ofsted or some other body, which seeks to identify strengths and weaknesses with a view to establishing priorities for improvement. The most common example is the school's financial audit (which is not a matter of choice); others often include the *Every Child Matters* agenda or element of provision. It is entirely up to the school how much of this approach it wants to use, but it is much better done as part of a planned, regular cycle of some aspect of the school's provision rather than as a big one-off event that may get a cynical response.

- **The external review approach** – where a school calls upon its 'critical friends' such as university partners and researchers, the LA and education consultants to review a particular aspect of the school's work and make recommendations for improvement. The SIP can carry out part of this role, but sometimes there is a need for a specialist approach in areas where the school itself lacks expertise and is not sure of the quality of provision.

- **The performance management approach** – this should be integral to one of the school's key management systems, but in good schools it is used not just as an annual appraisal of staff but as an ongoing focus of evaluation where it matters most: the quality of teaching and learning.

- **The benchmarking approach** – where the performance of the school is compared to that of other similar schools through performance and value added tables or local/regional families of schools' data such as that provisioned by City Challenge Programmes in London, Greater Manchester and the Black Country. This information is useful for self-evaluation only when the school takes positive action by contacting and visiting other schools whose results and practice is better than its own. Of course the same school is keen to act as host to other schools to explain their own good practice. This stimulates further reflective dialogue between schools and is a spur to further school and system improvement.

> Give enquiry and reflection pride of place.
>
> Stoll, Fink and Earl (2003)

- **The case-study/action research approach** – where the school's capacity for innovation and improvement is reflected in its strong culture of professional reflection and its practical case-studies. Some of these may be published externally, but are often published internally, and all of which bear testimony to an active, reflective, intelligent school community geared to school improvement. Schools like this often have a partner in higher education to help them research and evaluate. This approach to self-evaluation is much rarer than the other approaches and is the hallmark of a good and outstanding school.

Summary

Good schools have embedded the process of self-evaluation into all aspects of their work and therefore have an inbuilt momentum of school improvement. They don't wait for Ofsted inspections or set-piece occasions to evaluate how well they are doing as they are in the business of continuous school improvement. Their SEF is never completed but is constantly being amended and updated. The whole-school community knows how to

- collect and collate evidence
- analyse causes and solutions
- learn together to implement the quality of provision
- action-plan for new and better practice
- build capacity for change
- use critical friends to assist in evaluation.

The quest is restless and relentless. As one head said to us, 'When Ofsted came I didn't self-rate anything as "outstanding", but mainly good and a few things as satisfactory. Our in-school definition of "outstanding", as I explained to HMI, is that we are "best in class" but we never know what that could be.' Probably this school has gone beyond the normal systems of audit, analysing strengths and weaknesses, and action-planning towards striking a balance between 'appreciative enquiry' and 'problem-solving' (see Chapter 4).

Finally, in collective review the wise school realizes it is embedding continuous change and development. So at the end of the process of 'identifying practices for review', 'relating those prescribed to existing policies', 'collecting evidence' and finally 'evaluating the evidence, the policy and the practice with a view to action', the successful school adopts what one school calls the CAT process. That is, it decides what needs

- consolidating
- adjusting
- totally transforming.

The more successful a school is, the more it finds itself 'adjusting' most of what it does.

Reality check 2: Present preoccupations and future possibilities

As we have remarked elsewhere, the very successful school has to juggle the past, the present and the future. Ignore any one of these and you are on the short road to trouble. In fairness, both the past and more especially the present are difficult to ignore.

> It's juggling all these three components, however, that marks out the continually outstanding school: it never thinks it has 'arrived'. For the outstanding school if 'it ain't broke' it is just the very time to start fixing it. The outstanding schools anticipate.

As we saw in the first 'reality check' there is no shortage of present crisis, especially for the challenged school. Whatever the school, whether challenged or not, the present needs of the pupils and staff do not permit much time for future speculation: there are events to organize and attend; exams and tests to enter, set and mark; musical occasions, sports festivals and matches; lessons to give and observe; appointments to make. The list goes on. Yet we know we have to anticipate and handle the external agenda of constant change that rains down on us, some of it as we know ill-thought-out or frankly inappropriate. Ideally we want to shape that to our needs in order to have a sense of being in charge, instead of at the mercy, of events.

So as a second and concluding 'reality check' we set out some of those present and future issues in the hope that what we write now will have some present and future usefulness – and not appear immediately dated. We identify six issues.

1 The return of the curriculum

There was a time when we used to look for proof of capacity to innovate in the curriculum as a key factor in making headship appointments. We reckoned that if the head was interested in curriculum change then the more creative would be the teachers, with the desirable outcome of better pupil motivation, engagement and learning. Conversely of course, we were less likely (so we thought) to appoint a dull conservative preoccupied with simply maintaining the school as it was. System-maintainers and status-seekers is how we described them.

That was the pre-1988 mindset of headship-appointing panels. The National Curriculum changed all that. Everything curricular was prescribed and, in an Ofsted-regulated world, the last thing you wanted was someone who would rock the curriculum boat by taking unjustified risks, or worse still by putting their heads in the sand and pretending, as some briefly did, that the National Curriculum hadn't really happened.

Of course in those days, and since, we were still seeking heads who would take a professional lead rather than fall into the trap, as some people suggested they should, of becoming a 'chief executive' who managed the budget and the organization. Some of us thought therefore that the only way of securing a similar liveliness of mind in headteachers was to look for people who would take a professional lead in setting the tone for teaching and learning and other aspects of school improvement. We thought that was the way we could be sure of appointing someone who, like the curricular innovator of previous years, was aware of the need continually and tirelessly to promote the intellectual curiosity and therefore the liveliness and energy of the staff.

> Well it's time to declare that the National Curriculum as we knew it has no clothes. The 1988 overprescribed National Curriculum to all intents and purposes is no more. It's dead.

Now primary headteachers, prompted both by the DfES booklet urging *Excellence and Enjoyment* (2003) and by the Qualifications and Curriculum Authority curriculum review, are working out how best to secure creativity within the curriculum without putting at risk their SAT scores at age 7 and 11. One of the devices most heads and schools are using is to reintroduce the once reviled 'topic', usually in the form of a theme lasting either a week or, through apportioning time to it regularly each week, several weeks or a whole term or year. The justification is to capture the children's interest through working at a theme in-depth, which would necessarily involve them using investigation while simultaneously developing their basic skills of literacy, numeracy and ICT as well as their knowledge of some of the Foundation subjects such as history, geography, religious education, art, technology and science. In the hands of good teachers the 'topic' approach can be inspiring, but it suffers from one historical drawback – its name. It's surely only a matter of time before the wheel turns and critics mount an attack on 'topics' or 'projects' similar to that which occurred prior to the introduction of the dead and stultifying hand of the National Curriculum.

It seems to us that those schools that have called their approach 'research' and 'enterprise' themes are on a safer wicket. There is of course the political presentational reason. After all, who can argue with children being engaged in and acquiring the rudimentary disciplines of 'research' or taking part in 'enterprises'? However, there is also a more serious purpose. 'Research' will cause those engaging in it to agree ground-rules that will serve the purpose of encouraging the capacity of children to learn for themselves – the elusive 'learning to learn' purpose of education. The research we are talking about requires careful preparation. In one school we know, one of the deputies/assistants has a clear responsibility for 'research', not merely in the curriculum but among staff. So far as pupils are concerned, the school has debated how much of their research will be 'individual' and how much 'collective'. They realize the need to discuss the skills, habits and dispositions they are expecting their pupils to develop and display. The research requires carefully planned time in and out of school. (Out of school we are impressed by how schools use the focus on topics/research as a major element of 'homework'.) By 'planned' we mean a reconsideration of the timetable so that large chunks of time – occasionally a week or even several weeks – are devoted to extended and in-depth intensive learning, whether in the interests of research or the development of other life-skills, for example through residentials. At its best, as with all learning, the use of a research approach encourages teachers to ask skilful questions and seek to model an example through their own behaviour.

In short, we think that the primary school with an eye to the future will adopt a 'research' approach and we hope the professional associations, the Qualification and Curriculum Authority (QCA) and the GTC, will take the opportunity to promote the debate. What worries us is that central government will be tempted to lay down prescriptive rules that would be counterproductive to the creation of that form of intellectual curiosity which is one of the vital features of the outstanding school.

As for the secondary curriculum, we believe it is already undergoing enormous change and will experience yet more as a result of three initiatives.

The first initiative is relatively modest, namely the Royal Society of Arts *Opening Minds* project, which seeks in Key Stage 3 to challenge 'subject'-dominated thinking. Based on an analysis of desirable present and future skills, the *Opening Minds* schools have shown how a smaller group of teachers than is usual for Year 7 pupils to meet can successfully cover what's needed in Key Stage 3. One school, St Johns in Marlborough, has experimented with half the year group taking the *Opening Minds* approach and the other half being taught traditionally. A similar approach, though based on a theory of active learning and teachers involving their pupils in 'co-production', has been pioneered by the Hamlyn Foundation in a scheme called *Musical Futures*.

The second set of new thinking, which is closely allied to that of the RSA, has been provided by the QCA. It has sought a rethink of the Key Stage 3 curriculum – and in fairness the Key Stage 2 curriculum too – along similar lines, namely a more explicit focus on common skills and vital experiences that are shared across the various subject boundaries. Meanwhile the DfES dispensation to complete Key Stage 3 in two rather than three years has prompted many secondary schools either to adopt a primary-style approach for Year 7, followed by two intensive years to Key Stage 3 tests, or to start with two years and then proceed to Key Stage 4 early.

The third development also affects secondary schools. They are individually and sometimes collectively trying to make sense of the 14–19 agenda in the wake of the Tomlinson Report and the DfES response to it. Of course, most secondary schools realized some years ago that the National Curriculum was inappropriate for some of their students, with its emphasis on a common curriculum experience for all students in Key Stage 4. Up to a third of the age group needs something different from three core and seven foundation subjects, all terminating in an exam at 16, where five or more higher grades in GCSEs have become the holy but unattainable grail for this group of students. Therefore, they have either sought official dispensation or quietly forgotten the National Curriculum requirements, preferring to organize a variety of sandwich courses involving students attending college or work in companies or community voluntary projects for two or three days a week in Years 10 and 11. As such initiatives have spread and taken root, schools have universally reported greater motivation, better behaviour and attendance.

As more than one school has reported:

> Once youngsters have caught the bug of being interested in something beyond school which they can see as being useful to their future, perhaps in a place of work where they are the only youngster among adult company, they can see why a certain competence in the basics such as English, maths and ICT is worth working for – not least because their would-be employer is telling them so.

The introduction of the range of 14–19 diplomas in the next few years is an associated vital key development. It's hoped that they will represent another option to be considered alongside the present mix of GCSEs and BTECs that most schools have adopted in the light of the GNVQ changes. Whether these diplomas are acceptable rests on the content and its acceptability by commerce and industry. Most successful schools, as we write this, are in principle making movements towards the partnerships (with colleges and other schools) that will be necessary to deliver the full menu of diplomas but remain open-minded, if not yet completely convinced, about the prospect. After all, they have seen more false starts in this aspect of education than almost any other. One has only to mention Dearing or Higginson or the Schools' Council to older colleagues, and Tomlinson to those who have joined the profession more recently, to cause raised eyebrows about the DfES certainty about the timescales intended for the diplomas. Nevertheless, they are a necessary step *en route* to getting something worthwhile for all youngsters, not just those with an academic leaning. Something like them would have to be in place if the Tomlinson proposals for an overarching diploma are one day to become a reality.

It seems to us that the diplomas, or something like them, are this time likely to happen. The reason is to do with economics. In the developed world, governments are keenly aware that the future for their indigenous population individually and collectively hangs on ever higher standards of education and training just to keep up with the accelerating changes in our runaway world. The changes are stimulated by the explosion of information, technology and knowledge that, when coupled with global movements of peoples and capital, demand great creativity on the part of individuals and societies if they are anxious to keep up. Of course this proposition, resting as it does on a continuation of the market, will cause long moral debate among the more thoughtful! But schools faced with doing their best for the future citizens, who are their present students, know they have to accept reality even while arguing for something better. Politicians face the same dilemma. They know that the projections for our economy for 2020 suggest the need for 16 million rather than the present nine million graduates for jobs that require graduate qualification. More seriously there will be a yet further decline in the number of unskilled jobs from the present two million or so to just a few hundred thousand. The first challenge is easily met; there is no shortage of school- and college-leavers capable of filling the gaps. The second is much more serious, not least for that group of 10 or 11 per cent of youngsters who leave school and are then not in education, employment or training – the so-called NEETs. How do we avoid continually creating a group of adults who are increasingly alienated and disengaged and who don't identify with the rest of society? It's a problem that becomes the greater when the inevitable and accelerating migration of peoples from the poorer parts of the world is factored in. Such asylum-seekers, refugees and economic migrants will inevitably fill some of all the jobs available.

In such a world of increasing uncertainty we want youngsters to feel the future is theirs to seize and make sense of. It's why, therefore, secondary schools include thinking about the curriculum on their agenda in a way they haven't since 1988.

2 The international dimension to schooling

There is one further linked aspect of curriculum thinking that is acquiring greater importance in the vision of primary and secondary schools alike which are aspiring to developing outstanding success. That is internationalism. An ostrich-like preoccupation with 'Britishness', important though that is, might also encourage an insularity of approach that would be fatal for the interests of our future citizens. It is clear to all pupils in our larger (and some of our smaller) urban areas that the present population is multiracial, multifaith and multilingual. Individual pupils, moreover, have a multiple, not single, identity. In such areas teachers and schools do their best to build greater understanding between different points of view and different cultures. They do so for a complex web of reasons, the first of which is the process of teaching and learning itself. Teachers and schools know that it's vital that pupils know they value and empathize with the reality of their individual pupils' worlds, whether it's a matter of faith, language or cultural tradition. In other words, it's a vital ingredient in personalization. However, they do so too because they are often only too keenly aware that beyond the school gate mistrust is rampant among some elements of the adult community. As one head remarked to us, 'It's at times like this that I realize the extraordinary prescience of H.G. Wells' remark that "history is a race between education and catastrophe".'

The international dimension has prompted an increasing number of schools to change many aspects of their organization, not just the taught curriculum. It becomes a feature of every member of staff's job-description. It's a part of 'performance management or development' in opportunities for fresh experiences and targets of action agreed for the following year, just as it is of faculty or phase plans. In at least two schools we know the house system has been revamped to incorporate names that reflect the continents, and in another the achievements of great people from different parts of the world. In many it takes the form of making international links using the new possibilities of ICT. In at least one it's taken the form of a triangular link so that the well-placed partner school in their developing country makes the arrangements to facilitate the building of a primary school in another part of their country where no such provision is yet available. The money required to carry out the project is the focus of the British school's charitable efforts. Another is planning to send the very best equipment from their existing school, when they get Building Schools for the Future (BSF) new buildings, to their long-standing partner in Africa. Needless to say they are sending their students to help install the equipment . . . and do a lot of other things besides! One can imagine many schools adopting a similar approach during the next ten years or so of BSF. Many too are using the upcoming London Olympics in 2012 to make existing youngsters feel special as they seek to reinforce the personal best philosophy that drives all Olympian competitors, while at the same time using the interest generated to strengthen the international dimension.

However, the need for an international dimension to the curriculum has other roots, not least those we have already mentioned involving global interdependence such as diseases (for example AIDS), sustainability and the environment, as well as economic well-being. These are resolvable only though interdisciplinary cooperation and international collective action. We think Howard Gardner (2006) put the need for a new approach to curricular action well:

Understanding of the global system. The trends of globalization – the unprecedented and unpredictable movement of human beings, capital, information, and cultural life forms – need to be understood by the young persons who are and will always inhabit a global community. Some of the system will become manifest through the media, but many other facets – for the operation of worldwide markets – will need to be taught in a more formal manner.

Capacity to think analytically and creatively within disciplines. Simple mastery of information, concepts, and definitions will no longer suffice. Students will have to master disciplinary moves sufficiently so that they can apply them flexibly and generatively to deal with issues that could not be anticipated by the authors of textbooks.

Ability to tackle problems and issues that do not respect disciplinary boundaries. Many – perhaps most – of the most vexing issues facing the world today (including the issue of globalization!) do not respect disciplinary boundaries. AIDS, large-scale immigration, and global warming are examples of problems in need of inter-disciplinary thinking. One could take the position that it is first necessary to master individual disciplines; moving among or beyond disciplines then becomes the task of tertiary or professional education.

However, there is much to be said for beginning the process of inter-disciplinary work at an earlier point of education – as is done, for example, in the 'theory of knowledge' course required of students in the International Baccalaureate or the courses in 'problem-based learning' taught at the Illinois Mathematics and Science Academy. How best to begin to introduce rigorous multi-perspective thinking into our classrooms is a challenge that we have only begun to confront, and, as noted, our psychological understanding of the mind of the synthesizer has yet to coalesce.

Knowledge of and ability to interact civilly and productively with individuals from quite different cultural backgrounds – both within one's own society and across the planet. Globalization is selecting for interpersonal competencies, including the ability to think and work with others coming from very different racial, linguistic, religious, and cultural backgrounds . . . Mastery and cultivation of these competencies will be the cornerstone of educational system in the most successful democracies of the twenty-first century . . .

Knowledge of and respect for one's own cultural tradition(s). The terrorists who crashed into the twin towers of the World Trade Center in September 2001 privileged the scientific and technical knowledge and cognitive skills that globalization makes accessible. At the same time, they despised the Western (and especially the American) values, ethos, and world view that in many regions of the world – including much of western Europe – pass as globalization's underside. Societies that nurture the emergence of the instrumental skills needed to thrive while not subverting or undermining the expressive domains of culture – values, world views, and, especially, the domain of the sacred – will endure and may even have the edge in globalization's new regime. Managing the dual process of convergence (in the instrumental domains of culture) and divergence (in the expressive domains of culture) may well be among the most critical tasks of education for globalization. Societies that can manage this psychic ju-jitsu will thrive.

Fostering of hybrid or blended identities. Education for globalization will select for the crafting and performing of hybrid identities needed to work, think, and play across cultural boundaries . . . These will be increasingly indexed by multilingual competencies and transcultural sensibilities that will enable children to traverse discontinuous cultural meaning systems, to metabolize, decode, and make meaning in distinct, sometimes incommensurable cultural spaces and social fields. Societies that privilege transculturation and hybridity will be in a better position to thrive, while societies that enforce a regime of compulsive monoculturism and compulsive monolingualism are likely to lose out under globalization's emerging regime.

Fostering of tolerance. Education for globalization will give those societies that tend to (1) tolerate or, better yet, privilege dissent, (2) foster healthy scepticism, and (3) provide equality of opportunity, a powerful edge over societies that tend a privilege reflex-like consent and inequality of access to opportunity due to various ascribed qualities. More ominously, our world is unlikely to survive unless we become far more successful at fostering tolerant attitudes within and across nations.

(Gardner 2006, pp. 223–5)

This passage underlines the earlier points made about the need for curricular innovation as well as bringing a renewed focus on the future. We end this section therefore with a case-study concerning the future and drawn from experience abroad.

Case-study

In more than one American High School there is time set aside for what's called 'future problem-solving'. Put simply, groups of youngsters are presented with a problem that, on the best available evidence, seems likely to occur within either the USA or elsewhere in the world within the next 20 to 30 years. They are then asked, with appropriate prompting/coaching, to work in groups – and on occasions singly – in order to come up with solutions and consider a range of future contemporary events should the eventuality happen rather than be 'headed-off at the pass' as it were. Unsurprisingly, enthusiasts report much-increased student interest and learning. It leaves us wondering if there are some schools that are already involved in extending the same idea to an international group using ICT.

---

3 'Extended and full-service schools' and 'children's centres'

The 'extended school', the few 'full-service extended schools' and 'children's centre' agenda springs from a national thrust to shift some of the responsibility of 'care' from the family to the school. In the traditional school students are in school for 15 per cent of their waking time. The balance of 85 per cent is spent in the home and the community. Demographic trends have changed over the last 50 years: there are more older and fewer younger people of working age, as well as an increase in both parents in a family working. Small wonder that the state has recently created policies and practices to reflect these changed circumstances. Inevitably the school is centrally involved. School has always been a convenient place for parents to put their children while they worked. (After all, the the first elementary schools were located close to the factories and works where both working-class parents worked in the industrial age of the nineteenth century. Perhaps it's only a matter of time before some schools are built in the heart of the 'business', 'science' and 'light industrial' parks that today provide so many employment opportunities!) The school's childcare function lies at the heart of the 'extended school' development and is at least part of the reason for the creation of 'children's centres'. The second will command more time and attention of schools than the first. The opportunity that a 'children's centre' provides to help poorer and more challenged families to realize their hope of being 'good enough' parents has already stimulated promising innovative practices.

Along with health-service colleagues, some schools have become vital facilitators and natural working locations for the 'first-time parent health-visitor', the 'community parenting service' and the Foundation-stage staff, so that full advantage is taken of the precious time between birth and the Early Years in school. In some cities the shortage of speech and language specialist workers has prompted the creation of workers similar to the 'teaching assistant' development in school. As one grateful Manchester head remarked a few years ago,

> It's better to have someone who can give the one-to-one attention to the youngster and vitally the parent, even if she isn't the fully qualified speech and language therapist, than to be told there are none available. Moreover, if they live locally and are respected members of the community they are sometimes more acceptable than the expert who doesn't live here and know what it's like.

If a lot of time is devoted by the primary head to making the best of the local 'children's centre' less, at least of her personal time, will be given to 'extended school' although she will know in the end that it's her responsibility to make sure it happens and that the quality is concerned less with 'occupying children', as one head put it when shaking her head about the endless diet of DVDs in some after-school provision, as she explained her battle to secure provision that complemented and supplemented what happens in her school. Certainly many schools have widened and enriched their before- and after-school provision by using the talents and interests of all their staff, not just the teachers.

4 The challenge of the new technologies – ICT in school life

About Fifteen years ago the mobile phone was the size and weight of a half-brick. Virtually no pupils had access to them. Now every school has a policy shared with parents regarding pupil use of mobile phones – and a plethora of ICT-related activities for which we had no vocabulary ten years ago.

Some schools – soon it will surely be all – have an e-learning platform, which means that

- All pupils can access their homework, lesson-plans, videoed 'best explanations' of 'difficult to understand' concepts, computer-assisted learning programmes, school reports, timetables and individual coaching advice. They can text and are texted by their teachers.
- All staff can access the same list plus faculty and school management information, professional development portfolios, 'red', 'amber' and 'green' lists of pupil progress on a regular basis and a wealth of other useful information about pupils and curriculum.
- All senior leaders can access all the above and a range of management information relating to budget, performance of staff and pupils, and the detailed performance of other similar schools.
- All parents can access information about their own children's attendance, marks, reports and homework.
- Governors can access those parts of the above they have collectively agreed are appropriate to discharge their duties.

Every member of the school community has their personal space on this integrated system. It's part of the everyday way that the school community communicates and does its business. It can be accessed at any time, both in the school and remotely.

Of course the digital scene is forever shifting and bringing with it subtle changes and challenges to the way the school works: there is the need for constant adjustment if the school is to take full advantage of these changes. With the benefit of hindsight we should have rewritten Figure 2 on managing complex change (see p. 10), to demand that on every occasion the ICT implications are considered.

Schools are currently at different stages on the road to a system such as the one outlined above. They also know how to integrate within the system the various multimedia resources that enable the teacher to enrich their lessons when using either the interactive whiteboard or the computerized projector and screen. The digital pioneers will be using 'Fuse' to create their own curriculum.

Then there's the use of handheld devices, tablets and palm and laptops. In special schools and units the application of the technologies as a tool has overcome many learning barriers for those with moderate and severe learning difficulties and sensory and motor impairments. Outstanding schools know they need the staff with the intellectual curiosity and energy to keep abreast of – and sometimes lead – these developments.

The library, once the fortress-like exclusive preserve for the few, is now through the harnessing of the internet and the intranet within the e-learning platform the source of accurate and reliable information and knowledge for all. Moreover, these digitalized elements of the library are available at any time, both in school and remotely.

How is the outstanding school making sense of all this? There are probably four important ways they do so.

1 *Staff development*
Elsewhere in this book we have elaborated on the importance of continuous professional development. In ICT we have reached the stage where every faculty needs to keep its use of ICT under review. It will certainly be a key part of performance review/management and form a part of the departmental/phase self-reviews, as well as that of the school as a whole.

2 *Infrastructure*
The e-learning platform will greatly aid staff development for the obvious reason that it becomes part of the 'way we do things here'. It will also support and accelerate many changes in the work practices – for pupils as well as teachers and support staff. It requires school leadership to be alert to changes in available kit and issues of compatability and safety.

3 *Changes in practice in and out of school*
Successful schools acknowledge the fast-changing methods by which some young people learn and where they learn. As one digitally aware young teenager remarked cheekily, 'I don't let school get in the way of my education.' Beyond the school, some youngsters are acquiring skills of which their teachers are unaware. In order to overcome that some schools are adopting unconventional approaches: for instance one head told us that in Year 9 ICT lessons, students were allowed to lead the lesson with the express purpose of allowing those students in the vanguard of learning to share their skills and knowledge with other students and staff.

Additionally schools like this are alive to the issues of safety, which are discussed with pupils and parents.

4 *Understanding and supervising the use of ICT*
According to the excellent booklet *Their Space: education for the digital divide* from Demos (2007), there are eight myths that those of us charged with looking after the young need to explore. The first six, they categorize as 'moral panic':
- The internet is too dangerous for children.
- Junk culture is poisoning young people and taking over their lives.
- No learning happens and digital technologies are a waste of time.
- There is an epidemic of Internet plagiarism in schools.
- Young people are disengaged and disconnected.
- We're seeing the rise of a generation of passive consumers.

They counterpose these six with two myths they classify as 'digital faith':
- All gaming is good.
- All children are cyberkids.

Unless a school can debate these issues and arrive at an agreed position – and the Demos booklet will aid that – it is unlikely to navigate successfully the digital world.

The resolution of these issues helps to provide a guiding set of principles with which to face up to the accelerating changes.

We conclude this section with a useful glossary, also taken from the Demos booklet, as follows:

Bebo: a popular social networking site often for younger users with over 22 million registered members. It is estimated that five people register every second. (For schools it presents the issues of discussing safety since very few, if any, would allow school access, yet the reality is that a large proportion of their pupils' population will be accessing bebo outside school.)

Blog: a website that often takes the form of an online personal diary. The word blog is derived from web log and 'blogging' subjects are as varied as human interests.

Del.icio.us: a social bookmarking site. It enables individuals to save their favourite articles, blogs, music and reviews and share them with friends, family, coworkers and the del.icio.us community.

Facebook: a social networking site that uses corporate email addresses, particularly university emails, to verify users as members of already existing social networks and then becomes an extension of that network.

Flickr: a photo-sharing website. Not only an online photo album, its focus on the art of photography encourages and supports the growth of social networks through common creative interests.

GoogleVideo: similar to YouTube. It allows users to upload their own content, provides access to stock content and a marketplace for videos, music, TV episodes and trailers.

IMovie: a piece of software designed to make editing and producing professional-looking videos intuitively and quickly in order to reduce obstacles to home video creation.

IRC (Internet Relay Chat): a communication tool similar to MSN in that it allows the instant exchange of text messages. However, unlike MSN it allows strangers from all over the world to meet online and to communicate.

ITunes: music library management software that allows users to import music from CDs, organize it into playlists, play music, purchase it from an online store and load it on to their iPod.

MSN: one of a range of services that allows text messages to be sent from one computer to another instantly so that conversation can be carried out over the Internet.

MySpace: a fast-growing social networking site with over 100 million registered users globally. It offers an interactive, user-submitted network of friends, personal profiles, blogs, photos, music and videos.

Online international multiplayer games: take place in a computer-generated imaginary world. Players guide their custom-designed character through a virtual life. They are open-ended games that provide players with almost limitless possibilities. Popular examples include World of Warcraft and Secondlife.

Pizco: another social networking and blog site distinguished by its 'walled-garden' approach, protecting user privacy by not providing search facilities for users.

Podcasts: audio or video recordings that are downloaded automatically by software on subscribers' computers every time a new edition is posted on a website. Easy to produce and distribute, the customer can, and often does, turn creator.

Social networking: refers to the aspect of Web2.0 that allows users to create links between their online presence such as a web page or a collection of photos. These links may be through joining online groups or assigning direct links to other users through lists of friends or contacts.

Web 2.0: refers to a second generation of Internet-based services that emphasize online collaboration and sharing among users, often allowing users to build connections between themselves and others.

Wikis: websites where content can be edited by any visitor to the site. An example of a wiki is **Wikipedia** – an online encyclopedia providing free content to all visitors and to which any visitor can add their own information or make corrections simply by the 'edit this page' link.

YouTube: allows people to post their own videos for others to watch, to give their opinions on the content that is there and to make links between videos. Youtube has grown into an entertainment destination with people watching more than 70 million videos daily.

5 The use of data

It is frequently said that we live in a 'data-rich, information-poor' society. There's no doubt that the availability of data has never been better. It's how we use data that's important.

Schools are awash with data, much of it comparative. Such data are particularly useful to schools and parts of schools seeking to visit other schools – in comparable circumstances of pupil intake, of course – to learn how they do things: some better, some worse. Internally, such data are much more useful as a result of the work of the Fischer Family Trust: indeed it's fair to say that no teacher or department should be ignorant of the way some pupils with similar potential aren't learning in some areas but are in others. At the individual level, too, such data have the potential of enabling pupils 'at risk' to be pinpointed at the end of each year and can help to increase those pupils' competence, confidence and resilience next term.

Unless data are used by the leadership team of the school and directly related to the classroom, the school will remain information-poor. Some pupils will fail who need not do so. That will happen only when job-descriptions and habits of review are so framed that the data are used as a matter of course.

In the best schools, the development of the management and ICT-supported learning and communication techniques, as we have remarked above, has meant that management and learning information is available online, through a portal which can be accessed as appropriate by staff, pupils and parents.

Unless schools overcome their insularity, they run the risk of not finding ways to improve what they do. One of the features of outstanding schools is that they are always trying to find new and better ways of doing things. Often visits are not as useful as they could be because schools are so different. The Ofsted PANDA (performance and analysis), for example, leaves schools stranded, knowing that compared with the average of schools like them, they are either (in real terms or on value added) significantly above or significantly below others in comparable circumstances. However, they have no clue as to which those schools are. Given that most schools want to improve on their previous best such data are unhelpful – unless one knows the names of the schools in comparable circumstances, which are doing better and worse both in absolute terms and in the speed of improvement.

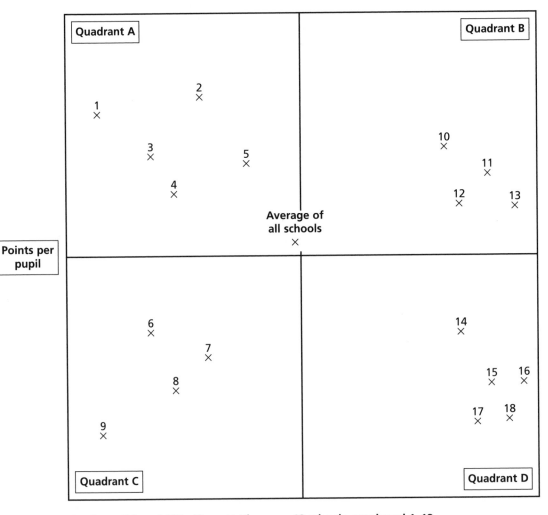

Key Stage 2,3 or GCSE   Key = ✕: There are 18 schools, numbered 1–18

Figure 5 Family of schools of similar socioeconomic background: rate of improvement over three years

That's why the 'family of schools' initiatives, at first in Birmingham and now in London, Greater Manchester and the Black Country are so important. The diagram above shows the format of how each family of schools is represented.

Quadrants

Clearly quadrant C schools have low performance and are not improving as fast as other comparable schools, perhaps 'not waving but drowning'? Quadrant A schools are improving more quickly but have low points per pupil, perhaps 'heads above the water'? Quadrant B are schools with high points per pupil and high rates of improvement, perhaps 'walking on water'? Finally, quadrant D schools have high points per pupil but low rates of improvement, perhaps 'treading water'? The point of the 'family' is that schools have similar prior entry attainment scores and similar numbers entitled to free school meals. So, schools do not need to waste time. They can visit and learn from schools they know to be broadly similar. When such data are added to the data from the Fischer Family Trust, there is the potential to learn from each other, subject by subject and with different groups of pupils.

The same approach within the school but with pupils' performance might enable departments to see much more clearly how their rate of improvement and absolute ability to help their pupils' development differs. Clearly such data would need to be handled with care, but almost all secondary schools are already using a positive and negative 'residual' approach to tackle the same issue.

6 New forms of leadership

Elsewhere in this book we have explored the implications of 'partnerships' for individual schools. Increasingly schools are forming variously 'loose' or 'tight' 'federations', 'collegiates' or 'partnerships'. There are two sorts: voluntary and imposed. The first typically occurs where a group of secondary schools or primary schools form a federation of equals, or a cross-phase partnership or pyramid serving together a local community. Essentially the voluntary nature of them can lead to too much informality and energy lost through being at cross-purposes. To be successful they need expressly to consider and agree such issues as

- purpose (for example ICT, professional development, curriculum, pupil-enrichment, shared facilities and so on)
- values (if not agreed the source of great tension)
- leadership (ideally shared and rotated)
- organization (whoever is going to be the progress-chaser/administrator will need resources)
- budget
- success criteria
- dates for honest review (ideally involving outsider).

Many schools now find themselves in more explicit and forced federations, often to help a challenging school overcome longstanding or acute difficulty. Some have a new breed of chief executive. The PriceWaterhouseCoopers report (2007) helpfully sets out the possibilities:

Models of school leadership

An important part of the present research involved examining different models of school leadership, and identifying the aspects of those models that have a positive impact on pupil performance. The evidence shows that although leadership behaviours are generally more important than leadership models, the development of new models can be one of the conduits through which the right leadership behaviours are fostered. We have framed our analysis of this in terms of the following five broad types of leadership models:

Traditional model – here the leadership team is comprised exclusively of qualified teaching staff and typically includes a headteacher supported by deputy and/or assistant heads. In our research, this model predominated in the primary sector but was also common, albeit to a lesser extent, in secondary schools.

Managed model – this model moves away from the traditional model towards a flatter management-style structure in which specific roles are allocated on the senior leadership team for senior support staff, for example, directors of finance and/or HR. This model tends to be found more often in the secondary sector with almost half of heads stating that they had one senior support staff member on the leadership team and a further 8 per cent stating they had two senior support staff members.

Multi-agency managed model – this model is a natural progression from the managed model and is, in a sense, born out of the imperatives of the *Every Child Matters* and 14–19 agendas. Like the managed model it involves a flatter, management-style structure, but is more outward-looking and inter-agency focused. It can manifest itself in a wide variety of ways, but generally will involve teaching staff and professionals from other agencies working together as part of school leadership teams. This model remains the exception rather than the rule but, as outlined above, our expectation is that more schools are likely to move in this direction as a key way of responding to the ECM and 14–19 agendas.

Federated model – this model is characterized by varying degrees of collaboration between schools and sometimes between schools and other providers, for example: 'whole town' approaches to schooling; shared strategic governing bodies, with executive heads overseeing several schools; and federations between schools, further education and work-based learning providers. In our survey, almost one in ten headteachers reported some sort of formal federation arrangement; and the majority of schools reported informal collaborations with other schools.

System leadership model – this model embraces all the different roles that heads can assume beyond the boundaries of their own school, that is those that contribute to the wider educational system at a local, regional or national level.

It includes, for example National Leaders of Education assuming roles that include providing advice to government and 'virtual heads' responding to schools facing specific challenging circumstances.

Although we have focused on these six issues, they are merely illustrations. Politicians and the media will ensure that overload is always with us, sometimes for good reason, often, however, as a response to some immediate issues highlighted in the press. We think that if schools have thought through their positions on these six issues and are true to their values they will thrive rather than survive – and that after all is the best means of ensuring that a good school becomes great.

Finally, we might add, the route to 'greatness' lies in moral purpose: the determination, brought to reality, that all members of the school community – teachers, support staff and pupils – should behave in a way that is mindful of each other. They will know what it is to feel grief and experience doubt as well as great joy. Above all they will know because they are the living example of it, that fairness lies at the heart of any civilized society, and they will see that reflected in the everyday actions of their school. A great school would embody the late Cardinal Basil Hume's summary of the purpose of education: 'We are not engaged in producing just good performaers in the marketplace or able technocrats. Our task is the training of good human beings, puposeful and wise, themselves with a vision of what it is to be human, and the kind of society that makes this possible.'

References

Abbot, John (1994) *Learning Makes Sense – Recreating education for a changing future*, Education 2000, Letchworth

Adams, Henry B. (1918) *The Education of Henry Adams*, Houghton Mifflin, Boston, MA

Ayers, William (1993) *To Teach: The journey of a teacher*, Teacher's College Press, New York and London

Barber, Michael (1996) *The Learning Game: Arguments for an education revolution*, Victor Gollancz, London

Barth, Roland S. (1990) *Improving Schools from Within*, Jossey-Bass, San Francisco, CA

Bastiani, J. (2003) *Involving Parents, Raising Achievement*, DfES Publications, Nottingham

Bentley, Tom (1998) *Learning Beyond the Classroom*, Routledge, London

Black, P., William, D. (1998) *Inside the Black Box: Raising standards through classroom assessment*, NFER–Nelson, London

Black, P., William, D. (2002) *Working inside the Black Box: Assessment for learning in the classroom*, NFER–Nelson, London

Blunkett, David (2000) *Raising Aspirations in the 21st Century*, DfES Publications, Nottingham

Brighouse, Tim (1991) *What Makes a Good School?*, Network Educational Press, Stafford

Brighouse, Tim (2006) *Essential Pieces: The jigsaw of a successful school*, Research Machines Publications, Abingdon

Brighouse, Tim (2007) *How Successful Headteachers Survive and Thrive*, Research Machines Publications, Abingdon

Brighouse, Tim and Woods, David (1997) *School Improvement Butterflies*, Questions Publications, Birmingham

Brighouse, Tim and Woods, David (1999) *How to Improve your School*, Routledge, London

Brighouse, Tim and Woods, David (2005) *Butterflies for School Improvement*, DfES Publications, (London Challenge), Nottingham

Brighouse, Tim and Woods, David (2006) *Inspirations – A collection of commentaries to promote school improvement*, Continuum, London

Bubb, Sara (2005) *Helping Teachers Develop*, Sage, London

Bubb, Sara and Earley, Peter (2007 2nd Edn), *Leading and Managing Continuous Professional Development*, Paul Chapman, London

Burke, C. and Grosvenor, I. (2003) *The School I'd Like*, Routledge/Falmer, London

Clark, D (1996) *Schools as Learning Communities*, Cassell, London

Claxton, G. (2002) *Building Learning Power: Helping young people become better learners*, T.L.O.

Clegg, Sir Alec (1980) *About our Schools*, Blackwell, Oxford

Collins, Tim (2001) *Good to Great*, Random House, London

Cooperrider, D. and Srivasta, S. (1987) 'Appreciative enquiry into organisational life', *Organisation and Development*, 1: 129–69

Green, H. and Hannon, C. (2007) *Their Space: Education for the digital divide*, Demos, London

Desforges, Charles, with Abouchaar, Alberto (2003) *The Impact of Parental Involvement, Parental Support and Family Education on Pupil Achievement and Adjustment: A literature review*, DfES Research Report 433

Dewey, John (1916) *Democracy and Education: An introduction to the philosophy of education*, Macmillan, New York

DfES (2003a) Every Child Matters, DfES Publications, Nottingham

DfES (2003b) Excellence and Enjoyment: A Strategy for primary schools, DfES Publications, Nottingham

DfES (2004) A National Conversation about Personalised Learning, DfES Publications, Nottingham

DfES (2004) Putting the World into World-Class Education, DfES Publications, Nottingham

DfES (2005) Learning Behaviour: The report of the practitioner's group on school behaviour and discipline, DfES Publications, Nottingham

DfES (2006) 2020 Vision – report of the teaching and learning in 2020 review group, DfES Publications, Nottingham

DfES (2006) Higher Standards, Better Schools for All, DfES Publications, Nottingham

DfES (2006) Making Good Progress, DfES Publications, Nottingham

DfES (2006) The Five Year Strategy for Children and Learners: maintaining the excellent progress, DfES Publications, Nottingham

DfES (2007) Making Great Progress, Schools with Outstanding Rates of Progression in Key Stage 2, DfES Publications, Nottingham

DfES/Ofsted (2004) A New Relationship with Schools: Improving Performance through School Self-Evaluation, DfES Publications, Nottingham

Drucker, Peter F. (1993) Post-Capitalist Society, Butterworth–Heinemann, Oxford. Repr. with permission from Elsevier

Einstein, Albert (1950) Out of my Later Years, Thames & Hudson, London. With kind permission of Philosophical Library Inc. New York

Eliot, A. (2007) State Schools since the 1950s: The good news, Trentham Books, Stoke-on-Trent

Fried, Robert L. (1995) The Passionate Teacher, Beacon Press, Boston, MA

Fullan, Michael (1991) The New Meaning of Educational Change, Cassell, London

Fullan, Michael (1993) Change Forces: Probing the depths of education reform, Falmer, London

Fullan, Michael (1999) Change Forces: The sequel, Falmer, London

Fullan, Michael (2001) Leading in a Culture of Change, Jossey-Bass, San Francisco, CA

Fullan, Michael (2003) Change Forces with a Vengeance, Routledge/Falmer, London

Fullan, Michael (2004) The Moral Imperative of School Leadership, Sage, London

Fullan, Michael (2005) Leadership and Sustainability, Sage, London

Gann, N. (1998) Improving School Governance, Falmer Press, London

Gardner, Howard (1991) The Unschooled Mind: How children think and how schools should teach, Basic Books, New York

Gardner, Howard (1995) Leading Minds: Anatomy of leadership, Basic Books, New York

Gardner, Howard (2006) The Education and Development of the Mind – Selected Works, Routledge, London

Gladwell, Malcolm (2000) The Tipping Point: How little things can make a difference, Little Brown, London

Gleeson, D. and Husbands, C. (2001) The Performing School, Routledge/Falmer, London

Goleman, D. (1996) Emotional Intelligence, Bloomsbury, London

Grey, D. (2005) Grey's Essential Miscellany for Teachers, Continuum, London

Handy, Charles B. (1994) The Empty Raincoat: Making sense of the future, Hutchinson, London

Handy, Charles B. (1997) The Hungry Spirit, Hutchinson, London

Hargreaves, A. and Fullan, M. (1992) What's Worth Fighting for in your School?, Open University Press/McGraw-Hill, Buckingham and London

Hargreaves, A. and Fullan, M. (1998) What's Worth Fighting for in Education?, Open University PressPress/McGraw-Hill, Buckingham and London

Hargreaves, D.H. (1982) The Challenge for the Comprehensive School, Routledge & Kegan Paul, London

Hargreaves, D.H. (1998) Creative Professionalism, Demos, London

Hargreaves, D.H. (2003) Working Laterally: How innovation networks make an education epidemic, DfES, London

Hargreaves, D.H. (2005) Personalised Learning, 4 & 5, SSAT, London

Hargreaves, D.H. (2006) A New Shape for Schooling?, SSAT, London

Hart, S., Dixon, A., Drummond, A.J. and McIntyre, D. (2004) *Learning without Limits*, Open University Press/McGraw-Hill, Buckingham and London

Hoffer, Eric (1998) *Vanguard Management*

Hopkins, D. (2001) *School Improvement for Real*, Routledge/Falmer, London

Jonson, B. (2003) *Ten Thoughts about Time: A philosophical enquiry*, Constable, London

Joyce, B., Calhoun, E. and Hopkins, D. (1999) *The New Structure of School Improvement*, Open University Press, Buckingham

Kao, John J. (1996) *Jamming: The art and discipline of business creativity*, HarperCollins, London

Kipling, R. (1902) *Just So Stories*, Macmillan, London. Reprinted by permission of A P Watt Ltd on behalf of the National Trust for Places of Historic Interest or Natural Beauty

Leadbeater, C. (2005) *The Shape of Things to Come*, DfES Publications, Nottingham

Little, Judith W. (1981) *The Power of Organisational Setting*, National Institute of Education, Washington, DC

MacBeath, J. (1999) *Schools Must Speak for Themselves*, Routledge, London

MacGilchrist, B., Myers K., Reed, J. (2004) *The Intelligent School* (2nd Edn), Sage, London

Maden, M. (ed.) (2001) *Success against the Odds, Five Years On*, Routledge/Falmer, London

Maden, M. and Hillman, J. (eds) (1996) *Success against the Odds*, Paul Hamlyn Foundation, Routledge, London

Margo, J., Dickson, M., with Pearce, N. and Reed, H. (2006) *Freedoms Orphans: Raising youth in a changing world,* Institute for Public Policy Research, London

McCourt, Frank (2005) *Teacher Man*, Fourth Estate, London

Morris, Estelle (2001) *Professionalism and Trust: The future of teachers and teaching*, DfES, Nottingham

Mortimore, P., Sammons P., Stoll, L., Lewis, D., Ecob, R. (1988) *School Matters*, University of California Press, Berkeley, CA

NCSL (2007) *Greenhouse Schools*, NCSL, Nottingham

NCSL (2007) *Leadership Succession: An Overview*, NCSL, Nottingham

Ofsted (2000) *Improving City Schools*, Ofsted, London

Ofsted (2003) *Boys' Achievement in Secondary Schools*, Ofsted, London

Ofsted (2005) *Remodelling the School Workforce*, Ofsted, London

Ofsted (2006) *Best Practice in Self-Evaluation*, Ofsted, London

Ofsted (2006) *Improving Performance through School Self-Evaluation and Improvement Planning*, Ofsted, London

Ofsted (2007) *Promoting Community Cohesion in Schools*, Ofsted, London

PriceWaterhouseCoopers (2007) *Independent Study into School Leadership*, DfES Publications, Nottingham

Riley, K.A. (1998) *Whose School is it Anyway?*, Falmer Press, London

Robinson, K. (2002) *Out of Our Minds: Learning to be Creative*, Capstone, Oxford

Senge, Peter M. (1990) *The Fifth Discipline: The art and practice of the learning organisation*, Doubleday, New York

Sennett, F. (2004) *400 Quotable Quotes from the World's Leading Educators*, Corwin Press, Sage, Thousand Oaks, CA, and London

Sergiovanni, T.J. (2001) *Leadership: What's in it for schools?*, Routledge/Falmer, London

Silver, H. (1994) *Good Schools, Effective Schools*, Cassell, London

Smith, Jonathan (2000) *The Learning Game: A teacher's inspirational story*, Little Brown, London

Stoll, L., Fink D. and Earl L. (2003) *It's about Learning and it's about Time*, Routledge/Falmer, London

Toffler, A. (1990) *Powershift*, Bantam Books, New York and London

Van Maurik, John (2001) *Writers on Leadership*, Penguin Business, London

West-Burnham, John and Coates, M. (2005) *Personalising Learning*, Network Educational Press, Stafford

White, R.C. (2000) *The School of Tomorrow*, Open University Press, Buckingham

Woods, D.C. and Cribb, M. (eds) (2001) *Effective LEAs and School Improvement*, Routledge/Falmer, London

Wragg, E.C. (2005) *The Art and Science of Teaching and Learning: The Selected Works of Ted Wragg*, Routledge, London

Index

Page numbers in *italic* refer to head-of-chapter and other quotations separate from the main text.

2 4 4 4